GARDENING
WITH
CLIMBERS

UNA VAN DER SPUY

GARDENING

WITH

CLIMBERS

CLIMBERS OF THE WORLD
FOR GARDENS
IN THE SOUTHERN HEMISPHERE
AND OTHER TEMPERATE REGIONS

PROTEA PRESS PUBLISHERS

Grow Beaumontia for its handsome leaves and lovely, lily-
like flowers.

Other books by the same author:

Gardening in Southern Africa
Ornamental Shrubs & Trees
Garden Planning & Construction
Wild Flowers of South Africa for the Garden
South African Shrubs and Trees for the Garden
Gardening with Shrubs
Gardening with Ground Covers

PROTEA PRESS PUBLISHERS
Box 254
Stellenbosch 7600
South Africa

ISBN 0 909065 02 0

Set in 11 on 12 pt Baskerville
Lithographic reproduction by Hirt & Carter (Pty) Ltd,
Cape Town
Designed and printed by Creda Press, Cape Town
Binding by Edward D. Seabrook (Pty) Ltd, Cape Town

Contents

I

Part I
Introduction

Mexican Blood Trumpet, known also as *Bignonia cherere* (*Phaedranthus*), is a vigorous climber with attractive foliage and magnificent flowers.

Introduction

Climbers are versatile and graceful plants which can enhance the garden in many ways. In fact, the entire atmosphere of a property can be transformed by draping the walls of the house with a curtain of colourful climbers, or by letting them romp up into a tree or spill gracefully over a bare bank or the edge of a balcony. They are indispensable plants for gardens large and small.

Climbers can provide the shade so desirable in the garden, and they are particularly useful in a country such as ours, where the sun shines brightly during most months of the year. They will camouflage unattractive outbuildings and change a carport or a dreary-looking garage into a bower of beauty. They will clothe a fence or neglected hedge with a pretty mantle of leaves and flowers, and they are excellent plants to grow to form a screen for privacy, or to hide a dry bare bank or steep slope.

How to choose climbers. Before making a selection of climbers it is important to consider where they are to be planted and for what purpose. If they are to be against the walls of the house, choose those which cling on their own or which are not too exuberant in growth. If they are to mask an ugly outbuilding or be near a pool, choose evergreen ones so that the outbuilding will not be visible in winter, and to avoid having leaves falling into the pool. If they are to shade a patio or terrace, however, select deciduous ones so that the sunlight can stream through onto the patio during the winter months.

It is desirable also to know something of the habit of growth of a climber before deciding whether it is suitable, or where to plant it. All climbers need some kind of support. In nature, those which are natural climbers attach themselves to other plants and climb up and over them. In the garden we can allow them to embrace neighbouring plants, but generally it is advisable to give them a suitable support, and to trim and train them.

Where to plant them and how to trim or train them will depend to some extent on the nature of their growth, and it is perhaps best to consider and divide them into four broad groups:

1. Some have aerial roots or suction pads which cling tightly to a surface, such as a wall or the bole of a tree. Ivy, Virginia creeper and the little climbing fig (*Ficus pumila*) are three plants of this nature which make a neat cover to a large expanse of wall, attaching themselves to the wall as they grow.

2. The second group includes the twiners and twisters. These need some assistance to keep them in place. They will twine their stems around a support or about themselves. Wisteria and honeysuckle are two plants of this type. Some of these are vigorous in growth and need regular trimming to keep them within bounds, and to prevent them from suffocating neighbouring plants or becoming a tangled mass. This is a pleasant and easy task if tackled as soon as it becomes necessary.

3. The third group of climbers are those which have tendrils which help them to make their way up a support – be it a trellis, pillars or posts, or other plants. The tendrils will wind around the support and keep the plant in

place. The passion flower is one of the many which have tendrils. If these are planted against a wall a suitable support must be attached to the wall for the tendrils to entwine.

4. This group includes plants which are scandent in habit. They are not true climbers but they have long stems which can be trained along supports. If they are not tied to a support they will flop around on the ground or over neighbouring shrubs. Climbing and rambler roses, plumbago and the potato creeper belong to this group.

HOW TO SUPPORT CLIMBERS

The type of support depends on what purpose the climbers are to serve. Are they to beautify an ugly house or hide outbuildings, to soften a bare expanse of wall, to provide shade over a patio or in any other part of the garden, or are they to form a high screen or hedge? Whatever type of support is needed let it be a good, strong, permanent structure and not one which will rot. The least satisfactory are the so-called rustic ones which collapse in a few years. Having erected a suitable support the climbers should be trained from the outset in the direction they are to grow. Do not bunch the stems together and tie them to nails on the wall. Nothing looks more hideous.

Rods: One of the best ways of supporting climbers which are to be trained to decorate the walls of the house is by using perpendicular metal supports. These can be galvanised iron water pipes or the reinforcing rods used by builders. Three or four of these spaced 45 to 60 cm apart, fixed so that they extend from beneath the ground up to the eaves of the house, make a practical, durable and neat support for climbers. (See illustration on page 18)

Wire-mesh: This is usually fastened to the wall to enable twining plants and climbers with tendrils to make their way up and across the wall. It also provides a support to which to tie the scandent plants which would flop if not supported. Mesh with a plastic coating is ideal because it cannot rust but, if this is not procurable, use the wire-mesh made for fencing, or that used by builders as reinforcing. A wire-mesh gate makes a good support but it is naturally somewhat more expensive than wire-mesh purchased by the metre.

Fix the mesh neatly to the walls of the house or any outbuilding which needs dressing up, but in doing so make sure that there is space between the mesh and the walls, to allow the tendrils to get a grip of the mesh or to provide space for tying the climbers to the mesh. The climbers will soon cover it completely.

Lattice or trellis: Thin lattice-work of wood is not recommended. It lasts for only a few years and generally collapses when the climber is well-grown, leaving one with the unpleasant task of starting all over again, to untangle the mess and train the climber anew. If a wooden support is to be used, let it be a trellis made of durable timber 2-4 cm thick, and be sure to procure wood that has been properly sealed or treated with a preservative, to prevent it from rotting, or paint it with a long-lasting paint. This kind of trellis can be used against a wall or fastened between posts so that the climbers can cover it and make a screen.

If wooden uprights or posts are to be used to support a screen or to form an arch or pergola, it is recommended that the wood be impregnated, and not merely painted, with a preservative. Wooden posts not impregnated usually rot off at ground level, not below the ground. Bed the posts down firmly into a concrete foundation set in the ground, and let the concrete project above the ground around the post to a height of about 6 cm to prevent the wood rotting at ground level. Otherwise anchor the wooden uprights by means of metal sockets or ties which project 6-10 cm above the ground and which go down into a concrete foundation. Seal or paint the wood to preserve its life. White is the best colour to apply to wood, wherever it is used in the garden, whether it be uprights, or crosspieces on a patio, or garden furniture. It is restful, yet forms a sharp, pleasant contrast to the different shades of green in the surroundings.

Screen: Climbers trained on a tall trellis of wire-mesh or wood make a more decorative screen than shrubs and trees, and, because they grow upwards rather than laterally, they take up less space, and are therefore more desirable plants for the small garden. The uprights at each end of the screen must be of durable material and very firmly embedded in the soil, as otherwise the force of wind against a well-grown climber may cause the uprights to keel over. In the small garden use metal or wooden uprights to support

Zimbabwe Creeper (*Podranea brycei*) is a robust climber for the large garden.

A screen covered by a climber. An effective way to ensure privacy.

Climbers not only add colour to the garden but they will shade the house and terrace.

the trellis. In the large garden pillars of brick or concrete will probably be more in scale and therefore more attractive, but even these can collapse if they are not well constructed and on firm foundations.

A screen draped with climbers is both decorative and useful. Erected around the perimeter of the property it makes the garden cosy and private. It protects the garden from wind, and it provides shade. It can be sited to separate one part of the garden from the other – e.g. the vegetable patch, work area or compost heap from the ornamental garden, or to hide any ugly feature on your own or a neighbouring property.

Arbour, patio and pergola: Pillars or posts decorated with climbers may be used to embellish the garden in different ways. A single pillar standing alone with a plant twined around it is seldom attractive and may look odd, but two, standing two to four metres apart joined by a crossbeam, will form a pleasant entrance to the garden or carport, and four, arranged in a rectangular fashion with crosspieces connecting them, will make a shady arbour – an attractive feature in any garden. To provide a canopy of shade for outdoor living on a terrace or patio erect uprights of metal, wood or brick the required distance from the house, to support a framework and crosspieces joined to the wall of the house. Such frames made of vinyl are now available for the purpose of supporting climbers to shade the patio or terrace. These have the advantage of being durable and they do not need painting. Furthermore they are so light and easy to handle that the home-owner can erect a frame of this kind in an afternoon. Climbers trained over a frame on supporting posts or pillars also make an attractive carport.

In a large garden pillars may be erected along both sides of a walk or drive to form a pergola where a variety of climbers may be displayed.

Whether the pillars or posts are to form an arch, arbour or pergola it is important that they should be an integral part of the general garden design and serve a definite purpose. They should not be erected just anywhere in a meaningless fashion. An arch could, for example, frame a view, introduce the path from the pavement to the house or lead from one part of the garden to another. An arbour could be the focal point at the end of the path, or it could be sited near the swimming pool to create a shady nook for those who are not swimming and for serving *al fresco* refreshments. In a large garden an arbour should be at a point where one is beguiled to rest and listen to the song of birds in the surrounding trees, or watch the play of light and the reflections in the water of an ornamental pool.

A pergola should always lead somewhere and not stand in purposeless isolation. In a large garden in a hot country, unless there are trees to provide shade as one walks around, it is a good idea to make a pergola to lead from one section of the garden to the next. The uprights should be placed so that there is a path at least 2 metres wide between them and they should be 2,5 metres or more in height. If the dimensions are less than this, there will be insufficient space for the climbers to grow and display their beauty whilst still allowing space for two persons to walk abreast along the pergola.

The pillars may be of wood, metal, concrete or brick. Uprights of wood or metal are most suitable for a small pergola whereas for a large one, pillars of brick or concrete look better. The space between the pillars along the sides of the path should be somewhat more than the width of the path. If the width is 2 metres, set the pillars at least 2,5 metres apart down each side. Attach crosspieces of treated or painted timber or metal on top of the pillars. The climbers can then be trained up the pillars and over the crosspieces to interlace overhead. In some cases a chain is attached from pillar to pillar so that the climbers can swing along on each side of the path, as well as interlace over the crossbeams.

Walls: The smaller the plot the more necessary it is to be restrained in planting. Some town gardens are so small that the area of the walls of the house is as large as the area of ground around the house. Obviously, it is a good idea to marry the house to the garden by using the walls as a background. Draped with sheets of sweet-smelling climbers such as jasmine, honeysuckle or wisteria, or with brilliantly coloured ones, such as bougainvillea, campsis or golden shower, they will contribute a great deal to the beauty of the garden. Choose the climber to suit the wall. On the east and south walls of the house plant those which like partial or open shade. On the other two sides plant the sun-lovers or those which like warmth.

When choosing your climbers consider also their manner of growth. Do not plant a solandra, which likes to flaunt its beauty over a wide area, on the walls of a small house. Select climbers, such as clematis which remain small, or those which grow slowly, or those which are easily trained and which can be restrained without spoiling their appearance. On the other hand, if you want smooth coverage on a high wall, choose ivy or Virginia creeper which do not have decorative flowers, but which have pretty leaves, and which adhere to the walls on their own. Or, if you want elegance and colour, grow those which twine or have tendrils and bear pretty flowers too. These, with a little training and trimming, will make a delightful show on a large expanse of wall.

Those gardeners who have a wall surrounding the garden can profit from this by transforming the whole wall into a colourful background to the lawn or paving which adjoins it. Should there be a pool in the vicinity plant only evergreens for this situation.

Fences and hedges: Some home-owners enjoy having the garden open to the street whilst others who like complete privacy have a screen all around their property. On a small plot, those who wish to be enclosed should erect a wall, fence, or trellis, on which climbers can be grown, as these take up less ground than does a formal hedge, they need less trimming and are more colourful. A wall helps to soften street noises as well as provide privacy, but a fence is less costly to erect than a wall, and within two or three years it will be so completely covered with climbers that the fence is no longer seen.

When planting climbers along a fence train them fanwise from the outset so that the laterals grow out horizontally, otherwise the bottom part of the fence will be bare. Space the climbers 1-4 metres apart, depending on the vigour of their growth. Many climbers grow rapidly, and it is advisable to spend a few minutes now and then trimming and training them so that they do not become a tangled mess along the fence. Generally it can be assumed that climbers with a dense mass of small leaves make a more attractive hedge or screen than those with large leaves. The jasmines with small glossy leaves and highly-scented flowers make a delightful screen if given a support, and, where frosts are too severe for them, a hedge of primrose jasmine (*J. mesnyi*), which has soft apple-green leaves and bright yellow flowers, will make the garden bright and gay. In the descriptions of climbers those suitable for hedges are indicated.

Climbers on trees and shrubs: Climbers, by their very nature, have an urge to go up, and it is very easy to clothe a sad and neglected old tree, or an ugly one, with a beautiful mantle of climbers. Shade-loving ones are the most suitable for a large tree, but even the sun-loving ones will make a lovely show high up in the branches, provided the shade below is not too dense. A sun-loving climber planted at the base of a tree looks for light and sunshine and will usually make its way up towards it. Never remove an ugly or dead tree in the garden without first trying to envisage what can be done to beautify it. Even a forlorn-looking tree stump that has been an eyesore for years can become a thing of beauty. Simply plant a climber to throw a bright robe around it.

Many climbers enjoy draping themselves over a dead tree stump or clambering up through living trees. What could be more beautiful than a wisteria clothing the top of a straggly pine with its sweetly-scented flowers, or silver lace vine (polygonum) throwing its lacy cloak about an ancient pear, or a bignonia embracing a tired cypress?

There is a general misconception about the danger of associating climbers and trees – a belief that the climbers will strangle the tree. This is not true. Even the much-maligned ivy seldom kills a tree and one would not plant it, or any other vigorous climbers, near a tree which looks beautiful standing alone. One would not grow a bougainvillea on a flowering peach, prunus or cherry, but a clematis or rose climbing up into their lower branches looks enchanting. Match a bougainvillea with an equally tough character, such as a well-grown erythrina (kaffirboom or flame tree), or pine.

The smaller climbers of restrained growth can happily be planted amongst shrubs. They will clamber over them and add to the beauty of the shrubs, provided they are not allowed to cover them entirely. Flame lily (Gloriosa), the scandent aloe (*A. ciliaris*), and the large-flowering clematis hybrids are three suitable plants to allow to scramble over shrubs. By training climbers to grow into trees and shrubs, or up a pillar, or along a fence with other climbers, one has the benefit of a long period of colour – the season when the tree or shrub flowers and the season when the climbers come into flower. For example, plant a rambling rose and a wisteria together to embrace a pillar or adorn a fence and there will be colourful flowers from late winter, when the wisteria starts flowering, to summer when the rose stops blooming.

Climbers as trees: In the small garden where there is no space for trees, climbers may be grown to form small weeping trees. Bougainvillea and wisteria are two which create an enchanting picture when trained in this way. To train them it is essential to have a sturdy umbrella-type of support 2-3 metres in height. Make sure that the support is firmly embedded in the ground – preferably in concrete – so that it does not keel over before the stem of the plant has grown strong enough to support its crown. Allow the plant to have only one main stem and train this up to the umbrella, tying it to the support in several places to keep it straight. Each year, as the main stem thickens, examine the ties and renew them when they appear to be wearing thin, or if they become too tight around the thickening stem. Cut out all side growth which shoots out below the umbrella-top, and head back the laterals which develop above the umbrella. In three or four years, when the single main stem has thickened, the laterals above the umbrella can be allowed to spread out further, and in a few years the plant will form a pretty little tree with a cascading top.

Should suitable metal umbrella-like supports not be available, a support can be made by welding or bolting crosspieces to a metal standard or galvanised water pipe, or a small circular laundry-drying frame may be used.

Climbers in containers: Climbers planted in containers can be used to ornament the interior of the house, or they may be placed on a balcony or verandah, a terrace or a patio to introduce colour and form.

Because even the vigorous ones do not become too large when planted in pots, it is possible to keep a range of pot-grown climbers in the back-yard, and to move them to decorate the house, the terrace or patio when they come into flower.

The climbers grown for indoor show should be those of restrained growth which are shade-loving or shade-tolerant, whilst those grown in containers outside may be shade- or sun-lovers, depending upon the situation they are to occupy. Plant them in good soil, water them adequately and give them nutrients two or three times a year. The easiest way to supply the nutrients is by using the fertiliser tablets made for pot plants. The size of the container used will depend on the plant and the situation. A small climber indoors can be planted in a pot with a top diameter of only 20 cm whereas a climber for outdoor show needs a much larger one – at least 40 cm in depth and diameter.

Weather is the most important factor affecting the growth of climbers in containers. During hot, dry windy weather the leaves transpire freely and it is most important that the soil in the container should not be allowed to dry out. This may necessitate watering the plants daily, whereas during cool, cloudy weather or during the rainy season they may need water only once or twice a week.

Good drainage is also essential to the health and vigour of plants in containers. If the water given cannot drain away the soil will become noxious and the plant will die as a result. See that there are three or four holes 1–2 cm in diameter in the bottom of the container, and cover the bottom with small, sharp-edged stones (such as those used in the making of concrete), or with coarse gravel. This will prevent the soil in the container from blocking the drainage holes.

Preparing the soil: Many climbers are fast-growers and will perform the miracle of trans-forming the bare plot into a colourful picture more quickly than other plants, but the speed of growth of plants is influenced by the soil in which they are planted, so, if the soil appears to be of poor quality, take the trouble to improve it before planting, to encourage rapid and healthy growth.

Giving a plant the right start in life is important. It makes the world of difference to the plant and to the amount of care required later. Most plants need fertile soil, rich in humus, to promote healthy development. Humus is a word used to describe decomposing vegetable matter and it includes compost and leaf mould. In nature humus is manufactured quietly and unobtrusively in field and forest. Grasses die off, weeds and wild shrubs and trees shed their leaves and these rot away, covering the soil year after year with a thin layer of humus. In the garden this does not happen. We rake up fallen leaves and take out weeds, and unfortunately we seldom turn them into compost, which is a great pity!

Having decided where to plant the climbers, make holes (round or square) at least 60 cm in width and depth and fill them with good compost, leaf mould or old stable manure, mixed with some of the top soil removed from the hole. If

Erect an arch for climbers to create an attractive entrance to the garden and home.

A handsome frame for climbers which will in time shade the terrace and house.

Bougainvillea in a container will highlight the garden, terrace or patio.

Trimmed bougainvillea forms a colourful, sturdy and impenetrable hedge.

A wall and frame for climbers to provide shade and privacy near a pool.

Wisteria can be trained to grow into an elegant small tree of weeping form.

Cup of Gold (Solandra) may rise to the top of a six-storey building.

Twine a rose around a pillar to introduce colour and form.

Here a climbing rose brings colour when the wisteria has finished flowering.

Climbers which flower at the same time can make a spectacular show. (Canary Creeper and Golden Shower).

perchance fresh manure is used make sure that it does not come into contact with the roots of the young plants. Mix it with soil in the lower 30 cm of the hole, and cover it with a thin layer of soil so that the roots will grow down into it in due course.

Compost is not a balanced food and gardeners all too often assume that, having put compost into the holes at planting time, they need do nothing more for the developing plants. Humus (compost, leaf mould or old manure) is a soil conditioner. It improves the texture of the soil and encourages the activity of the invisible organisms which promote soil fertility. As such it is most important and may be all that the plant requires, but it does not necessarily provide the plant with a balanced ration for the following years.

Observe the growth of the climbers and if, having planted them in good soil and watered them well and regularly, they appear to be ailing or not growing, apply a general garden fertiliser. Always water the soil before and after applying fertiliser so that it is diluted and more readily available to the plant. A tablespoonful sprinkled around the plant is usually sufficient. When applying fertiliser make sure that it is at least 20 cm away from the stems, as fertiliser touching tender new growth can burn it. For quicker results dissolve the fertiliser in a bucket of water, and water the ground around the plant with this.

It must be remembered that the rate of growth of plants differs to a marked degree. Some of the lusty ones will grow at such speed that you can almost see the stems elongating, whilst others are by nature slow, and, giving these extra food may not promote quicker growth. It should be remembered, too, that the growth of plants slows down in autumn and speeds up again in spring.

Generally the colour of the leaves is an indication as to whether a plant needs feeding. Plants are like humans in this respect. Pale green leaves, like pale wan cheeks, may indicate that the plant needs a pep-up in the form of extra nutrients. Those plants which like acid soil are, however, an exception, as their leaves become pallid when they are grown in soil which is alkaline, and a general garden fertiliser should never be given to them for it would only exacerbate the condition.

Should plants which like acid soil show yellowing of the leaves, apply a sprinkling of alum, sulphur or iron sulphate to the soil, and water it in, or spray the leaves with iron chelates. This is obtainable from garden centres, and directions for its use are given on the package. Peat which is basically acid does much to promote the growth of plants which prefer acid to alkaline soil. It has the advantage also of retaining moisture when once it has become thoroughly wet, but dry peat forked into soil may have a deleterious effect if the ground is not soaked immediately, as it will absorb, like a sponge, whatever moisture there is in the soil.

Time to plant: The general rule is that the deciduous climbers should be planted in winter, when they are bare of leaves and dormant or semi-dormant. Nurserymen grow deciduous plants in rows in the field and deliver them in winter time with a wrapping (not soil) about the roots, to prevent them from drying out. Such plants cost less than those in pots or plastic bags as they require less maintenance in the nursery, but all plants can now be procured from nurseries, established in containers of one kind or another. The general rule, however, still applies – namely, if possible plant the deciduous ones in winter. If, for any reason this is not possible, plant at any other time, but preferably during the rainy season.

Whether planting evergreen or deciduous plants, try to remove the plant from the container without disturbing the soil about its roots. This is not as difficult as it sounds, particularly with plants in plastic containers. Before trying to remove a plant from a container water it well and compress the soil by pressing firmly around the sides of the container, then cut down the sides of the plastic or, if it is another type of container which is not easily cut, turn it upside down and tap it on the bottom until the plant comes out with its soil firmly adhering around the roots. Place the plant in the hole so that the top soil level will be more or less the same as when it grew in the container, and, having done this, fill in the space around the rootball carefully, ramming the soil used to fill in the hole against the soil in which the plant is rooted. If this operation is done carelessly the soil invariably breaks away from the roots and, if it is a fussy kind of plant, it might show its resentment by dying back. At any sign of die-back after planting, cut back the stems of the plant to within 20 to 30 cm of the ground.

Always soak the ground thoroughly immediately after planting and, if the plant is in leaf and the weather is hot and dry, shade it, using a screen of wood, hessian or shade-cloth, or a leafy branch.

Frost: Climatic conditions in our country vary tremendously, the factors most limiting to growth being extremes of frost and dryness. Some plants are hardy to frost whilst others are tender and may be killed by even mild frost. Most of the climbers included in this book are reasonably hardy and will tolerate moderate frost, and some of them not only stand severe frost, but flower better in gardens subjected to sharp cold. Often a frost-tender plant can be persuaded to grow in a region which has frost, if it is protected for the first two to three years of its life. This protection may take the form of a tripod of stakes set firmly in the ground around the plant with a wrap-around covering of hessian, straw or plastic. In regions where the sunlight is intense avoid using plastic, or else take it off during the heat of the day, as it can result in too sweaty an atmosphere or scorching of the leaves. Hessian does not give as good protection against frost as straw, but it has the advantage of allowing more light to filter through to the developing leaves.

Gardeners living in regions of severe frost should make a point of growing those plants which are frost-hardy. Some plants which normally succumb to sharp frost can be grown successfully if planted where they have shelter from a wall, hedge or trees. In areas of severe frost, plants which flower in winter may have their flowers spoilt by frost, and it is therefore recommended that such plants be set out in a position where the first rays of the early morning sun will not strike the flowers. Shade until approximately 10 a.m. will usually obviate such damage, as the air which has warmed up will dissipate the frost on leaves and flowers before the sun shines onto them. Lists of climbers hardy to frost appear on pages 27 and 28.

Water: Each year we learn more and more about the requirements of plants, and the observant gardener will soon discover that water is one of the most important elements influencing growth. Retarded development is more often due to insufficient water than lack of nutrients in the soil. This is because plants absorb food only in soluble form. Therefore, no matter how much fertiliser is given, good growth may not result unless the plants are watered adequately.

It is impossible to lay down exactly how much water to give or how often, as this depends on the nature of the plant, the type of soil and weather conditions. Some plants enjoy fairly dry conditions and these are able to tolerate months of drought without flinching; others may not die, but they will look sad and dejected with wilting stems and leaves, and some will fade away altogether, if they do not receive enough water.

The intensity of the sunlight and the prevalence of drying wind are two factors which influence the watering programme, and make it necessary to water regularly and well all those plants which are not drought-resistant by nature.

Wherever possible soak the ground in the late afternoon or evening so that the moisture percolates to the roots of the plants, where it is most needed before the sun has a chance to absorb it, and, when hot winds blow, allow the sprinkler to play over the foliage during the day to help combat the rate of transpiration.

Those who live in regions where the rainfall is low or where there is an acute shortage of water should rely on climbers which stand dry conditions; or they should create shady and sheltered areas which will reduce the amount of watering necessary. A frame of wood or metal covered with shade-cloth will enable gardeners in very dry areas to raise plants which are not drought-resistant. Very often, also, the shade of a tree or the shade on the south side of the house will provide a good situation for a climber which is not resistant to long periods with little or no water. Choose a climber which tolerates or likes shade, to grow beneath a large tree. The tree itself absorbs water from the soil, but the nearer to the trunk the climber is planted the less likely it is to suffer from thirst because the feeding roots of trees are not near the trunk. It must be remembered however, that little rain reaches the roots of a climber near the bole of a tree with dense foliage. Climbers growing against the walls of the house may also suffer from dryness because the eaves of the house keep the rain off them. The easiest way to water climbers planted near the bole of a tree or against walls is to remove the sprinkler from the hose and to flood the soil around the plants once or twice a week.

In hot dry regions it is a good idea to mulch the ground over the roots of plants as this keeps the soil cool and retards the rate of evaporation of moisture from the soil. The mulch may be straw or chaff, or stones packed closely together over the root area.

Slender metal rods from ground to eaves make a firm support (*Clytostoma callistegioides*).

Enhance a large tree by planting a climber to flower in its branches.

Clematis – Nelly Moser – transforming the wall of a house into a sheet of colour.

The montana clematis looks delightful scrambling over shrubs and trees.

Plant one or more climbers to shade the patio, terrace and carport.

Clematis montana, with its flowers of white or pale pink, is the perfect embellishment for a wall.

Trimming and training: One cannot be definite as to the size to which a plant will grow, and the figures given for height and spread are those which a plant is likely to attain under good average conditions. Growth depends on climate, water, soil, the exposure, the nature of the plant, the knowledge of the gardener and the care he gives his plants. It often happens that, unless checked, climbers will grow too large for the space available for them on the walls of the house, or in any other position in the garden. They need a certain amount of trimming and training to keep them attractive.

The word trimming does not mean pruning. In pruning, the stems or canes are cut back in a specific way – old ones being cut off at an eye or growth-bud to encourage new growth to develop from that point. In trimming climbers (except climbing roses and a few others) the cutting back need not be done with precision, to a growth-bud or eye. In fact, a pair of hedge shears can be used on plants which are tangled, cutting them off on top and along the sides as far as is necessary, without paying any attention to eyes or growth-buds, as one would in pruning. Particulars are given in the text on those few climbers which require a specific method of pruning.

With most climbers the main trimming should be done immediately after flowering is over, but the plant will suffer no damage if this task is performed at any other time of the year. Cutting back a climber severely a couple of months before its flowering time may, however, reduce the number of flowers it bears that particular year.

Generally it is advisable to watch the growth of climbers, and, should they appear to be spreading too far and wide, snip off some of the tip growth whenever it appears to be necessary. Some of the exuberant climbers may also send up too many stems from the base. In this case remove, at ground level, those stems which appear to be unnecessary.

Nothing detracts more from the beauty of a climber than a tangle of bushy growth, but it is easy to avoid this happening by trimming the plants when necessary – with just a little snipping here and there. At the same time train the stems in the way you wish them to grow. If the climbers are to form a hedge train the stems laterally along a fence or the boundary wall of the property. If they are to embellish the walls of the house, train them either laterally, tying them to supports or special nails procurable for this purpose, or

attach them to perpendicular supports.

It is advisable at the outset to decide more or less how much space each climber is allowed to cover, as a single vigorous climber will cover the walls and roof of the house if it is not checked. Climbers with tendrils may need more frequent attention than those which have no such means of support. They very soon get themselves into a tangle because the tendrils cling to other parts of the climber or adjacent plants.

Climbers which are to adorn pillars or a pergola or patio will need much the same kind of trimming given to those along a fence or wall, but, in this case, the plants will be trained around the pillar or post and then over the crosspieces. To avoid having too much growth around the upright and too heavy a cover overhead, allow only three or four stems to develop from the base and tie these to the uprights as they lengthen, cutting out any other stems or canes which emerge from ground level.

Pests and diseases: Climbers are not subject to many pests and diseases, but in different areas and under certain climatic conditions they may suffer some damage as a result of an infestation. If action is taken as soon as a pest or disease becomes apparent their elimination is fairly easy.

Insect pests are broadly divided into two categories – those which chew the leaves or flowers (e.g. beetles and caterpillars) and those which suck the juices from stems, leaves or flowers, e.g. aphids.

Numerous effective sprays are procurable. These sprays, generally referred to as insecticides, are divided into three broad classes: contact, stomach and systemic. Contact insecticides kill on contact and are used against aphids and many caterpillars. Sprays which act on the stomach are for chewing insects such as caterpillars, beetles and other insects which eat the leaves, flowers or stems of plants. The systemic sprays do not remain as a residue on the surface of the plant but are absorbed into its sap, and they are effective against most insects – sucking and chewing ones.

Almost all insecticides are poisonous and should be kept out of the way of children and animals, and used strictly according to the directions given on the package. Unfortunately these insecticides kill off the natural predators which would in time consume the pests, and for this reason, they should be used only when other methods of control have failed. In the garden of normal size beetles may be caught and killed and aphids can be kept under control by running the fingers over the tips of the stems, thus removing them. Very often this, or a strong jet of water applied to that part of the plant where they are clustered, will be sufficient, and within three weeks, such action, plus their natural enemies, will eliminate them. Aphids are seasonal in their activity and appear in most gardens regularly every year. They (and other insects such as scale) are spread by the activity of ants and it is therefore advisable to destroy ants in the garden. Slugs and snails may also cause considerable damage to plants during damp, cloudy weather. These can be kept under control by using any of the baits sold for this purpose. Generally it is necessary to put down such baits once every week or ten days during periods when these pests are troublesome.

Diseases may do more serious damage to plants than insects, but few climbers are subject to them. The diseases most likely to affect climbers are the fungus ones such as rust, mildew, wilt and blackspot. Rust generally appears on the undersides of leaves as tiny, rusty-red spots. Mildew is characterised by a white or grey powdery substance on the tips of stems and leaves, and the leaves often show a tendency to curl up. Leaves which wilt for no apparent reason may be a sign that the plant is attacked by a fungus disease known as wilt. It is difficult to cure or eradicate, but there are several fungicides on the market which can be used for this and other diseases. Blackspot, which attacks roses and a few other plants, is more fully dealt with in the section on roses.

The artistic grouping of plants: The art of gardening lies in grouping plants in such a way that they combine happily to make a pleasing picture. Before purchasing climbers try to envisage what the final result will look like, and think out interesting colour schemes. Climbers flower at different seasons of the year and the garden should include some which flower during the different seasons, so that it will not appear bare at any one season. Before making a selection, evaluate the foliage of the plants, too, as flowers are of seasonal interest whereas foliage keeps the garden looking fresh and attractive throughout the year.

To enable the gardener to make a selection there are tables on pages 26 and 33 to 43, showing which plants have good foliage and which flower during the different seasons. These, together with the other tables, make it easy to choose climbers for different climatic conditions and to suit different positions in the garden.

Names: Many gardeners find that the botanical names of plants are difficult to remember, and this is not surprising because, being based largely on Latin and Greek, they look unpronounceable and they are seldom easy to spell. If one pronounces the names out aloud, syllable by syllable, it is however, surprising how quickly they begin to roll off the tongue. In this book the common names, where these exist, are given, but they are not altogether reliable since common names may differ from region to region, and they do not always describe the plant required. In order to avoid confusion and to obtain the right plant one should have the correct botanical name, that is the genus name (surname) and the species name (First or Christian name).

In addition to the genus and species names some plants have cultivar names. The word cultivar is now used instead of the word variety to describe hybrids grown in gardens. The cultivar name appears after the species name and is always written with an intital capital letter and in single inverted commas. It is often descriptive of some characteristic of the plant. For example, *Wisteria floribunda* 'Alba' is the name of a wisteria which has white flowers, *alba* being the Latin word for white.

Acknowledgements: To gardeners and horticulturists in my own country and in other countries I owe a debt of gratitude, for sharing their knowledge with me. One learns a great deal from those who garden under different climatic conditions and who encounter different problems.

Although most of the pictures are my own, the book is the richer for the contributions of those whose names are mentioned below: Mrs. Cynthia Giddy for pictures of Dipladenia, Mandevilla, Mucuna and Strongylodon; Mrs. Rosalind Redwood of New Zealand for pictures of *Clematis paniculata* and Quisqualis; Mr. P. Ayerst for pictures of Maurandia and Mr. T. Wannenburg for the picture on page 44.

I would also like to thank Mr. M. Lemmer of Rhodesia, a world authority on bougainvilleas, for his helpful advice, and Dr. John Rourke, Director of the Compton Herbarium, who was ever ready to check botanical names when asked to do so.

Part II
Plant Selection Guide

The pink form of *Pandorea jasminoides* makes a scintillating
show in mid-spring.

Plant Selection Guide

The tables which follow have been compiled to assist gardeners to choose the right climbers to suit their climatic conditions and to introduce variety in form and colour from season to season.

CLIMBERS

24

QUICK-GROWING CLIMBERS

Every home-owner longs to create a garden in the shortest possible time. This is understandable, and fortunately there are some decorative climbers to satisfy the most impatient of gardeners.

It must be remembered, however, when choosing plants for quick cover, that the plant could eventually prove too invasive, particularly if the plot is small. Be prepared, therefore, to remove the plant later on when the slow-growers have come into their own, or to trim the exuberant ones drastically, to keep them within bounds.

It is worth recording also that plants which are quick-growing in the right environment may sulk and refuse to make rapid progress if conditions are uncongenial. For example, a plant which likes warm conditions is unlikely to grow quickly where winters are cool and of long duration, and a shade-loving one may shrivel away if planted in a position where it is subjected to intense sunlight.

To ensure quick growth choose the right climbers for your climate and give them the growing conditions which they require, taking particular care to water them well and regularly during their first three years, and later on, too, when necessary.

Actinidia chinensis
Akebia quinata
Allemanda cathartica
Antigonon leptopus
Aristolochia species
Beaumontia grandiflora
Bignonia capreolata
Bougainvillea species
Calonyction aculeatum
Campsis species
Celastrus species
Cissus species
Clematis species
Clerodendrum splendens
Clytostoma species
Cobaea scandens
Combretum microphyllum
Congea tomentosa
Dipogon lignosus
Distictis species
Doxantha unguis-cati
Eccremocarpus scaber
Gelsemium sempervirens
Gloriosa species
Hardenbergia comptoniana

Hibbertia scandens
Ipomoea species
Jasminum (some species)
Kennedia species
Lablab purpureus
Lathyrus species
Lonicera species
Manettia bicolor
Pandorea species
Passiflora species
Phaedranthus buccinatorius
Phaseolus caracalla
Podranea species
Polygonum species
Quamoclit lobata
Quisqualis indica
Rhodochiton atrosanguineum
Rosa species and cultivars
Saritaea magnifica
Senecio species
Solandra species
Solanum species
Stictocardia beraviensis
Thunbergia species
Tropaeolum species

EVERGREEN CLIMBERS

Whether to choose an evergreen or deciduous climber depends largely on the position the plant is to occupy. If it is to camouflage an ugly house or hide outbuildings, to serve as a screen or to act as a hedge to ensure privacy, or if it is to provide shade next to a swimming pool, choose an evergreen plant. On the terrace or patio, where it is desirable to have sun in winter and shade during the other seasons, plant a deciduous one. If space permits grow one (or more) of each, otherwise the patio or terrace may look bare during the cold months of the year.

Plants with pretty foliage are marked with an *

*Acridocarpus natalitius
*Adenocalymma nitida
*Allemanda species
 Aloe ciliaris
 Anemopaegma chamberlaynii
 Antigonon leptopus
 Araujia sericofera
*Asparagus plumosus
 Asteranthera ovata
*Beaumontia grandiflora
 Berberidopsis corallina
 Bignonia capreolata
 Billardiera longiflora
 Bougainvillea species
*Chonemorpha macrophylla
*Cissus species
 Clematis (some species)
*Clerodendrum species
*Clianthus puniceus
 Clitoria ternatea
*Clytostoma species
 Cobaea scandens
*Cryptostegia grandiflora
 Dendromecon rigida
 Dipladenia splendens
 Distictis species
 Eccremocarpus scaber
 Eustrephus latifolius
*Ficus pumila
 Fremontodendron californicum
 Gelsemium sempervirens
 Hardenbergia comptoniana
*Hedera species and cultivars
 Hibbertia scandens
*Hoya species
 Hydrangea integerrima
 Ipomoea (some species)
*Jasminum (most species)

 Kennedia species
*Lapageria rosea
*Lonicera (many species)
 Luculia gratissima
 Manettia bicolor
 Maurandya barclaiana
 Metrosideros carminea
*Monstera deliciosa
 Mucuna bennettii
 Muehlenbeckia complexa
 Oxera pulchella
*Pandorea species
*Passiflora (some species)
 Petrea volubilis
*Phaedranthus buccinatorius
 Phaseolus caracalla
*Philodendron species
*Plumbago species
*Podranea species
 Porana paniculata
*Pyrostegia venusta
*Rhaphidophora aurea
*Rhoicissus tomentosa
*Ribes speciosum
*Saritaea magnifica
*Senecio species
 Solandra species
 Sollya fusiformis
 Stauntonia hexaphylla
*Stephanotis floribunda
*Stictocardia beraviensis
*Stigmaphyllon ciliatum
 Strongylodon macrobotrys
*Strophanthus gratus
 Tecomanthe venusta
*Tecomaria capensis
 Thunbergia (some species)
*Trachelospermum jasminoides

26

CLIMBERS WITH FRAGRANT FLOWERS

We are all inclined to expect a garden to be full of sweetly-scented flowers, and certainly scent does add much to the joy of a garden. Although the list of climbers with fragrant flowers is not a long one it is possible to have scented flowers during most months of the year by planting a selection from the climbers listed here.

Actinidia chinensis
Akebia quinata
Araujia sericofera
Beaumontia grandiflora
Calonyction aculeatum
Chonemorpha macrophylla
Clematis brachiata
Clematis flammula
Clematis tangutica
Distictis laxiflora
Doxantha unguis-cati
Dregea sinensis
Gelsemium sempervirens
Hoya species
Jasminum angulare
Jasminum azoricum
Jasminum beesianum
Jasminum dispersum
Jasminum multipartitum
Jasminum officinale
Jasminum polyanthum

Jasminum sambac
Lathyrus odorata
Lonicera caprifolium
Lonicera x americana
Lonicera hildebrandiana
Lonicera japonica
Lonicera periclymenum
Luculia gratissima
Mandevilla laxa
Oxera pulchella
Phaseolus caracalla
Porana paniculata
Quisqualis indica
Rosa (some species and cultivars)
Senecio tamoides
Solandra maxima
Stauntonia hexaphylla
Stephanotis floribunda
Strophanthus gratus
Trachelospermum jasminoides
Wisteria species and cultivars

CLIMBERS HARDY TO SEVERE FROST

A few regions of the country experience such severe frost as to limit considerably the range of plants which can be grown. Fortunately, climbers which are only half-hardy will often survive severe winters if protected during their first three years, and if they are grown against a wall, or in the shelter of other plants such as trees or shrubs. Walls retain warmth and protect plants from damage by cold wind. Shade from the early morning sun also mitigates frost damage. The plants listed here will stand the most severe frost. The names of less hardy plants, many of which will endure severe cold when established, appear in the next list.

Actinidia species
Akebia quinata
Ampelopsis brevipedunculata
Berberidopsis corallina
Bignonia capreolata
Billardiera longiflora

Campsis species and cultivars
Ceanothus species and cultivars
Celastrus species
Clematis (species and cultivars)
Clianthus puniceus
Clytostoma callistegioides

Dendromecon rigida
Doxantha unguis-cati
Dregea sinensis
Eccremocarpus scaber
Ficus pumila
Fremontodendron californicum
Gloriosa species
Hardenbergia comptoniana
Hedera species and cultivars
Hydrangea species
Jasminum beesianum
Jasminum floridum
Jasminum mesnyi
Jasminum nudiflorum
Jasminum officinale
Jasminum x stephanense
Laburnum vossii
Lapageria rosea
Lonicera x americana

Lonicera x brownii
Lonicera caprifolium
Lonicera x heckrottii
Lonicera japonica
Lonicera periclymenum
Lonicera sempervirens
Lonicera x tellmanniana
Lonicera tragophylla
Muehlenbeckia complexa
Parthenocissus (all species)
Polygonum aubertii
Polygonum baldschuanicum
Ribes speciosum
Rosa species and cultivars
Schizophragma species
Stauntonia hexaphylla
Trachelospermum jasminoides
Vitis species and cultivars
Wisteria species and cultivars

CLIMBERS WHICH STAND MODERATE FROST

The climbers mentioned in the previous list are also suitable for gardens which experience only moderate frost. The word moderate is used to include gardens where the drop in temperature at night is seldom more than −3° C. Where temperatures a little lower than this occasionally occur the top-growth may suffer but the roots usually survive.

Acridocarpus natalitius
Adenocalymma nitida
Aloe ciliaris
Antigonon leptopus
Araujia sericofera
Aristolochia species
Asparagus plumosus
Beaumontia grandiflora
Billardiera longiflora
Bomarea species
Bougainvillea (some cultivars)
Cissus species
Clematis brachiata
Clytostoma species
Cobaea scandens
Combretum microphyllum
Cryptostegia grandiflora
Dipladenia splendens
Distictis species

Gelsemium sempervirens
Gloriosa species
Hibbertia species
Ipomoea (some species)
Jasminum (many species)
Kennedia species
Lapageria rosea
Lathyrus species
Mandevilla laxa
Maurandya barclaiana
Metrosideros carminea
Pandorea species
Passiflora (some species)
Petrea volubilis
Phaedranthus buccinatorius
Phaseolus caracalla
Plumbago auriculata
Podranea species
Pyrostegia venusta

Rhoicissus tomentosa
Senecio macroglossus
Solandra species
Solanum (some species)
Sollya fusiformis

Stigmaphyllon ciliatum
Tecomaria capensis
Thunbergia (some species)
Tropaeolum speciosum

CLIMBERS FOR TROPICAL AND SUBTROPICAL GARDENS

Gardeners in tropical and subtropical regions are somewhat restricted in the range of trees and shrubs which can be grown, but a wide diversity of most beautiful climbers flourish under such climatic conditions. Their problem will not be one of protecting plants to encourage growth, but that of restraining the exuberant development of some of the climbers which enjoy a mild climate. Cutting back or training climbers once or twice a year is, however, not an onerous task.

Adenocalymma nitida
Allemanda species
Aloe ciliaris
Antigonon leptopus
Araujia sericofera
Aristolochia elegans
Asparagus plumosus
Beaumontia grandiflora
Bomarea species
Bougainvillea cultivars
Calonyction aculeatum
Chonemorpha macrophylla
Cissus species
Clerodendrum species
Clitoria ternatea
Cobaea scandens
Combretum microphyllum
Congea tomentosa
Cryptostegia grandiflora
Dipladenia splendens
Distictis species
Eustrephus latifolius
Ficus pumila
Gloriosa species
Hardenbergia comptoniana
Hibbertia scandens
Hoya species
Ipomoea species
Jasminum (some species)
Mandevilla laxa

Manettia bicolor
Maurandya barclaiana
Monstera deliciosa
Mucuna bennettii
Oxera pulchella
Pandorea species
Passiflora species
Petrea volubilis
Phaedranthus buccinatorius
Phaseolus caracalla
Philodendron species
Plumbago species
Podranea species
Porana paniculata
Pyrostegia venusta
Quisqualis indica
Rhaphidophora aurea
Rhoicissus tomentosa
Saritaea magnifica
Senecio species
Solandra species
Solanum species
Stephanotis floribunda
Stictocardia beraviensis
Stigmaphyllon ciliatum
Strongylodon macrobotrys
Strophanthus gratus
Tecomanthe venusta
Thunbergia species
Tropaeolum species

CLIMBERS FOR DRY GARDENS

No plants – not even succulents – enjoy being left completely dry throughout the year. Plants need water primarily because they absorb nutrients only in a soluble form and, if they receive no water they are starved – not just thirsty.

Some of the plants which are not drought-resistant by nature will do well in dry gardens if they are watered well during their first three to four years, that is until they have established a good root system. Such plants will also grow in dry areas if the texture of the soil is improved by the addition of plenty of compost, and if the ground around their roots is mulched.

Akebia quinata
Aloe ciliaris
Ampelopsis brevipedunculata
Asparagus plumosus
Bougainvillea cultivars
Clytostoma species
Combretum microphyllum
Dendromecon rigida
Distictis species
Dipogon lignosus
Doxantha unguis-cati
Ficus pumila
Gloriosa species
Hardenbergia comptoniana
Hedera species
Ipomoea (some species)

Jasminum (some species)
Kennedia species
Muehlenbeckia complexa
Pandorea species
Parthenocissus species
Phaedranthus buccinatorius
Plumbago auriculata
Podranea species
Polygonum species
Pyrostegia venusta
Senecio species
Solanum species
Tecomaria capensis
Thunbergia alata
Trachelospermum jasminoides
Vitis species

Plant a variety of climbers to create colour and interest from season to season.

Campsis produces its lovely curtain of flowers during the summer months. (*C. grandiflora*).

CLIMBERS FOR COASTAL GARDENS

Coastal gardens may prove difficult for one or more of three reasons. First, in gardens situated near the shore the salt in the air will inhibit the growth of most plants. Secondly, coastal winds are often strong enough to damage plants, and, if the wind is salt-laden it will be even more disastrous to plant growth. A third factor which makes coastal gardening difficult is the texture of the soil. Sandy soils generally lack humus and, unless the plants are given a good start, they are unlikely to flourish.

Lovely gardens are, however, to be found in many coastal towns where the soil has been improved by the addition of plenty of compost and/or manure, and where barricades have been erected to shelter young plants. Such shelters can be constructed around each climber, or the entire garden may be enclosed by a wall or a strong wire-mesh fence threaded with reeds or brushwood. Quick-growing climbers planted in the lee of the fence will soon hide it from view.

Plants likely to stand some salt in the atmosphere are marked with an *

*Acridocarpus natalitius
Adenocalymma nitida
*Allemanda species
*Aloe ciliaris
Antigonon leptopus
Asparagus plumosus
Beaumontia grandiflora
Bomarea species
Bougainvillea cultivars
Calonyction aculeatum
*Clerodendrum splendens
Clitoria ternatea
*Clytostoma species
Cobaea scandens
Congea tomentosa
*Cryptostegia grandiflora
Dipladenia splendens
*Ficus pumila
Gloriosa superba
Hardenbergia comptoniana
*Hedera species
Hibbertia scandens
Hoya species
Ipomoea species
Jasminum species
Mandevilla laxa

Maurandya barclaiana
Monstera deliciosa
*Muehlenbeckia complexa
Oxera pulchella
Pandorea species
Parthenocissus species
Passiflora species
Petrea volubilis
Phaedranthus buccinatorius
*Philodendron species
*Plumbago species
*Podranea species
Polygonum species
Pyrostegia venusta
Quisqualis indica
*Rhoicissus tomentosa
Senecio species
*Solandra species
*Solanum species
Stephanotis floribunda
Strongylodon macrobotrys
Strophanthus gratus
*Tecomaria capensis
Thunbergia (some species)
Tropaeolum species

CLIMBERS FOR SHADY PLACES

Shade differs in degree and quality from place to place even in the small garden. The south side of a building has open shade along the wall all day and, if it happens to be painted white, there is likely to be sufficient reflected light to grow sun-loving climbers against it. If it is a dark wall plant a shade-loving climber to cover it. An east-facing wall is shady in the afternoon whilst a west-facing one is shady in the morning.

The shade cast by trees varies considerably too. An evergreen with dense foliage casts heavy shade whilst a tree with sparse or finely-cut foliage provides the filtered light which some plants love. A large number of climbers do well when planted at the base of a tree so that their feet are shaded but their tops are in the sunlight.

Shade-loving climbers which will grow in full shade are marked with an *. The others will do well with morning sun and afternoon shade or in filtered shade.

Acridocarpus natalitius
Actinidia species
*Akebia quinata
Aloe ciliaris
Ampelopsis brevipedunculata
Aristolochia species
*Asparagus species
*Asteranthera ovata
*Berberidopsis corallina
Billardiera longiflora
Bomarea acutifolia
Calonyction aculeatum
Celastrus species
Chonemorpha macrophylla
Cissus species
Clematis species
Clerodendrum species
Clianthus puniceus
Clytostoma species
Dipladenia splendens
Distictis species
Eccremocarpus scaber
*Eustrephus latifolius
*Ficus pumila
Gloriosa species
Hardenbergia comptoniana
*Hedera species and cultivars

Hibbertia scandens
*Hoya species
*Hydrangea species
Jasminum (some species)
Laburnum vossii
Lapageria rosea
Lonicera species
Luculia gratissima
Manettia bicolor
Metrosideros carminea
*Monstera deliciosa
Mucuna bennettii
Muehlenbeckia complexa
Parthenocissus species
Phaedranthus buccinatorius
Philodendron species
Rhapidophora aurea
*Rhoicissus tomentosa
*Schizophragma species
Stauntonia hexaphylla
Stephanotis floribunda
Stigmaphyllon ciliatum
Strongylodon macrobotrys
Thunbergia (some species)
Tropaeolum (some species)
Wisteria species and cultivars

COLOUR THROUGH THE SEASONS

Although foliage plays an important part in the garden for most months of the year, flowers have a significant role to play, too, in highlighting the garden with colour from season to season.

In the lists which follow the flowers are classified under eight basic colours as a guide. A plant which bears flowers of in-between shades is listed under the colour which is nearest to it. For example, those with cream flowers are listed under white, and those with cyclamen flowers may be given under either pink or red, depending on which of these two colours predominate.

Where a plant is listed under two or more colours it does not always mean that it bears flowers of different colours but that its flowers may include more than one colour. For instance, some flowers are coloured red on the outside and yellow on the inside and would therefore be listed under both yellow and red.

33

The time when plants flower varies according to local climatic conditions. In regions where winters are mild many plants which normally flower in spring will come into flower in late winter. Because of the differences in climatic conditions prevailing in different parts of the country the following dates are used in this book to cover the seasons:

Spring	September to November
Summer	December to February
Autumn	March to May
Winter	June to August

The height given is an indication as to the size the climber is likely to attain under congenial conditions. They can be kept to smaller size quite easily by trimming them back as soon as they appear to be growing too large for their position in the garden.

SPRING

NAME OF PLANT	Height	Yellow	Orange	Red	Pink	Blue	Mauve	Purple	White
Actinidia kolomikta (KOLOMIKTA VINE)	3–4 m								●
Adenocalymma nitida (YELLOW TRUMPET)	6–10 m	●							
Allemanda species (ALLAMANDA, GOLD VINE)	2–4 m	●							
Aloe ciliaris (CLIMBING ALOE)	2–3 m			●					
Aristolochia species (DUTCHMAN'S PIPE)	3–6 m	●					●	●	
Beaumontia grandiflora (HERALD'S TRUMPET)	2–6 m								●
Bignonia capreolata (CROSS VINE)	6–10 m	●		●					
Bougainvillea cultivars (BOUGAINVILLEA)	3–9 m	●		●	●		●	●	●
Ceanothus (CALIFORNIAN LILAC)	2–3 m						●		
Clematis species & cultivars (CLEMATIS)	1–6 m					●	●	●	●
Clerodendrum species (CLERODENDRUM, BLEEDING HEART)	1–6 m			●					●

34

NAME OF PLANT	Height	Yellow	Orange	Red	Pink	Blue	Mauve	Purple	White
Clianthus puniceus (PARROT'S BILL, RED KOWHAI)	1–3 m			●					
Clytostoma species (PURPLE BIGNONIA, ORCHID TRUMPET)	6–9 m						●	●	
Combretum microphyllum (BURNING BUSH)	6–9 m			●					
Congea tomentosa (LAVENDER WREATH)	4–6 m						●	●	●
Dendromecon rigida (BUSH POPPY)	2–3 m	●							
Dipladenia splendens (DIPLADENIA)	3–4 m				●				
Distictis species (VANILLA TRUMPET VINE)	4–8 m						●	●	
Doxantha unguis-cati (CAT'S CLAW CREEPER)	4–10 m	●							
Fremontodendron californicum (FREMONTIA)	2–3 m	●							
Hardenbergia comptoniana (AUSTRALIAN PEA VINE)	3–4 m						●	●	
Hibbertia scandens (GUINEA GOLD VINE)	3–5 m	●							
Jasminum (most species) (JASMINE)	2–6 m	●							●
Kennedia species (CORAL VINE, TWINING PEA)	2–4 m			●				●	
Laburnum vossii (LABURNUM)	4–6 m	●							
Lathyrus species (SWEET PEA)	2 m			●	●		●	●	●

NAME OF PLANT	Height	Yellow	Orange	Red	Pink	Blue	Mauve	Purple	White
Lonicera (most species) (HONEYSUCKLE)	2–8 m	●		●	●				●
Mandevilla laxa (CHILEAN JASMINE)	3–10 m								●
Manettia bicolor (MANETTIA)	2–3 m	●		●					
Monstera deliciosa (DELICIOUS MONSTER)	3–4 m								●
Mucuna bennettii (FLAME OF THE FOREST CREEPER)	4–8 m			●					
Oxera pulchella (OXERA)	2–3 m								●
Pandorea species (BOWER VINE, WONGA-WONGA VINE)	4–6 m								●
Petrea volubilis (PURPLE WREATH)	4–8 m						●	●	
Phaedranthus buccinatorius (MEXICAN BLOOD TRUMPET)	4–9 m			●					
Phaseolus caracalla (SNAKE VINE)	3–5 m						●	●	
Rhodochiton atrosanguineum (PURPLE BELLS)	2–3 m							●	
Ribes speciosum (FUCHSIA-FLOWERING CURRANT)	2–3 m			●					
Rosa species & cultivars (CLIMBING AND RAMBLER ROSES)	2–4 m	●		●	●				●
Saritaea magnifica (SARITAEA)	6–10 m							●	
Solandra species (CUP OF GOLD)	4–10 m	●							

SPRING

NAME OF PLANT	Height	Yellow	Orange	Red	Pink	Blue	Mauve	Purple	White
Stictocardia beraviensis (MADAGASCAR CONVOLVULUS)	6–9 m	●		●					
Strongylodon macrobotrys (JADE VINE)	3–10 m		Green						
Tecomanthe venusta (TECOMANTHE)	1–3 m			●					
Thunbergia species (BLACK-EYED SUSAN, SKY FLOWER)	3–9 m	●	●	●					
Trachelospermum jasminoides (STAR JASMINE)	4–6 m								●
Wisteria species & cultivars (WISTERIA)	6–20 m				●		●		●

SUMMER

NAME OF PLANT	Height	Yellow	Orange	Red	Pink	Blue	Mauve	Purple	White
Acridocarpus natalitius (FEATHER CLIMBER)	2–3 m	●							
Anemopaegma chamberlaynii (YELLOW TRUMPET VINE)	6–9 m	●							
Antigonon leptopus (CORAL CREEPER, HONOLULU CREEPER)	4–10 m				●				
Aristolochia species (DUTCHMAN'S PIPE)	6–12 m	●					●	●	
Asteranthera ovata (ASTERANTHERA)	2–3 m			●					

NAME OF PLANT	Height	Yellow	Orange	Red	Pink	Blue	Mauve	Purple	White
Berberidopsis corallina (CORAL PLANT)	2–3 m			●					
Bomarea species (BOMAREA)	2–3 m	●		●					
Bougainvillea cultivars (BOUGAINVILLEA)	3–9 m	●		●	●		●	●	●
Calonyction aculeatum (MOONLIGHT CONVOLVULUS)	6–10 m								●
Campsis species (CHINESE TRUMPET CREEPER)	5–6 m	●	●	●					
Chonemorpha macrophylla (MALAYAN JASMINE)	5–10 m								●
Clematis brachiata (TRAVELLER'S JOY)	4–6 m								●
Clerodendrum splendens (CLERODENDRUM)	4–6 m			●					
Cobaea scandens (CATHEDRAL BELL, CUP-AND-SAUCER VINE)	3–4 m						●	●	
Combretum microphyllum (BURNING BUSH, FLAME OF THE FOREST)	6–9 m			●					
Distictis riversii (ROYAL TRUMPET VINE)	4–8 m						●	●	
Dregea sinensis (DREGEA)	2–3 m								●
Eccremocarpus scaber (CHILEAN GLORY FLOWER)	4–5 m	●		●					
Eustrephus latifolius (WOMBAT BERRY)	3–4 m				●				●
Gloriosa species (FLAME LILY, GLORY LILY)	2–4 m	●		●					

SUMMER

NAME OF PLANT	Height	Yellow	Orange	Red	Pink	Blue	Mauve	Purple	White
Hibbertia scandens (Guinea gold vine)	3–5 m	●							
Hoya species (Wax flower)	2–4 m				●				●
Hydrangea petiolaris (Climbing hydrangea)	4–6 m								●
Ipomoea species (Morning glory, cardinal creeper)	3–9 m			●		●	●	●	
Jasminum (some species) (Jasmine)	2–6 m								●
Lapageria rosea (Chilean bellflower)	2–3 m			●					
Mandevilla laxa (Chilean jasmine)	3–10 m								●
Maurandya barclaiana (Maurandia)	2–3 m							●	
Metrosideros carminea (Rata vine)	2–6 m			●					
Mucuna bennettii (Flame of the forest creeper)	4–8 m			●					
Pandorea jasminoides (Bower vine)	4–5 m				●				●
Passiflora (some species) (Passion flower, granadilla)	4–12 m			●			●	●	
Phaedranthus buccinatorius (Mexican blood trumpet)	4–9 m			●					
Phaseolus caracalla (Snail vine)	3–5 m						●	●	
Plumbago auriculata (Plumbago)	2–3 m					●			

39

NAME OF PLANT	Height	Yellow	Orange	Red	Pink	Blue	Mauve	Purple	White
Podranea species (PORT ST. JOHN'S & ZIMBABWE CREEPER)	6–9 m				●				
Polygonum species (RUSSIAN AND SILVER LACE VINE)	6–12 m			●					●
Quisqualis indica (RANGOON CREEPER)	3–4 m			●	●				●
Schizophragma species (CLIMBING HYDRANGEA)	6–9 m								●
Senecio species (CANARY & MEXICAN FLAME CREEPER)	3–5 m	●	●						
Solanum species (COSTA RICAN NIGHTSHADE, POTATO CREEPER)	2–6 m						●	●	
Sollya fusiformis (BLUEBELL CREEPER)	2–3 m					●			
Stigmaphyllon ciliatum (GOLDEN VINE, AMAZON VINE)	2–3 m	●							
Strongylodon macrobotrys (JADE VINE)	3–6 m		Green						
Tecomaria capensis (CAPE HONEYSUCKLE)	2–3 m	●	●						
Thunbergia grandiflora (SKY FLOWER)	3–4 m						●		●
Tropaeolum species (CANARY BIRD VINE, FLAME CREEPER)	2–3 m	●		●					

NAME OF PLANT	Height	Yellow	Orange	Red	Pink	Blue	Mauve	Purple	White
Actinidia chinensis (CHINESE GOOSEBERRY)	4–10 m		●						
Antigonon leptopus (CORAL CREEPER, HONOLULU CREEPER)	4–10 m				●				
Bomarea species (BOMAREA)	2–3 m	●		●					
Bougainvillea cultivars (BOUGAINVILLEA)	3–9 m	●		●	●		●	●	●
Calonyction aculeatum (MOONLIGHT CONVOLVULUS)	6–10 m								●
Campsis species (TRUMPET CREEPER)	5–6 m	●	●	●					
Eccremocarpus scaber (CHILEAN GLORY FLOWER)	4–6 m	●		●					
Eustrephus latifolius (WOMBAT BERRY)	3–4 m		●						
Ipomoea species (MORNING GLORY, CARDINAL CREEPER)	3–9 m			●		●	●	●	
Luculia gratissima (LUCULIA)	2–3 m				●				
Mandevilla laxa (CHILEAN JASMINE)	3–10 m								●
Maurandya barclaiana (MAURANDIA)	2–3 m							●	
Metrosideros carminea (RATA VINE)	2–6 m			●					
Mucuna species (FLAME OF THE FOREST CREEPER)	4–8 m			●					
Parthenocissus species (BOSTON IVY, VIRGINIA CREEPER)	4–12 m	Autumn leaves							

NAME OF PLANT		Yellow	Orange	Red	Pink	Blue	Mauve	Purple	White
Passiflora (some species) (Passion flower, granadilla)	4–12 m			●			●	●	
Plumbago species (Plumbago)	2–3 m				●	●			
Podranea species (Port st. john's & zimbabwe creeper)	6–9 m				●				
Polygonum aubertii (Silver lace vine)	6–12 m								●
Porana paniculata (Snow creeper)	6–10 m								●
Pyrostegia venusta (Golden shower)	4–8 m		●						
Senecio species (Canary & mexican flame creeper)	3–5 m	●	●						
Solanum species (Costa Rican nightshade, potato creeper)	2–6 m						●	●	
Strongylodon macrobotrys (Jade vine)	3–6 m	Green							
Tecomaria capensis (Cape honeysuckle)	2–3 m	●	●						
Thunbergia (some species) (Lady's slipper, sky flower)	3–4 m	●	●				●		●
Tropaeolum species (Canary bird vine, flame creeper)	2–3 m	●		●					
Vitis species (Japanese crimson vine & others)	3–12 m	Autumn leaves							
Wisteria species & cultivars (Wisteria)	3–10 m	Autumn leaves							

NAME OF PLANT	Height	Yellow	Orange	Red	Pink	Blue	Mauve	Purple	White
Aloe ciliaris (CLIMBING ALOE)	2–3 m			●					
Aristolochia californica (CALIFORNIA DUTCHMAN'S PIPE)	3–4 m	●						●	
Bougainvillea cultivars (BOUGAINVILLEA)	3–9 m	●		●	●		●	●	●
Clitoria ternatea (BLUE PEA VINE)	3–6 m					●	●		
Dendromecon rigida (BUSH POPPY)	2–3 m	●							
Gelsemium sempervirens (CAROLINA JASMINE)	3–4 m	●							
Jasminum mesnyi (PRIMROSE JASMINE)	3–5 m	●							
Kennedia nigricans (KENNEDIA)	2–3 m							●	
Monstera deliciosa (DELICIOUS MONSTER)	3–4 m								●
Porana paniculata (SNOW CREEPER)	6–10 m								●
Pyrostegia venusta (GOLDEN SHOWER)	4–8 m		●						
Ribes speciosum (FUCHSIA-FLOWERING CURRANT)	2–3 m			●					
Stauntonia hexaphylla (JAPANESE STAUNTON VINE)	3–6 m								●
Wisteria species and cultivars (WISTERIA)	3–10 m				●		●		●

Part III
Descriptions and Culture

The foliage colour of Virginia Creeper (Parthenocissus) adds
lustre to the garden in autumn.

Descriptions and Culture

ACRIDOCARPUS NATALITIUS
Feather Climber, Acridocarpus
Description: A scandent shrub rather than a true climber, this South African plant looks effective when trained against a wall or fence. Once vigorous growth has been established thin out some of the stems at the base and fasten the others flat against a wall, so that the beauty of the leaves and flowers can be the better displayed. It grows to 2–3 m and has glossy, oval pointed leaves which remain ornamental throughout the year. In summer pretty conical spikes of sulphur-yellow flowers make a gay sight against the background of lustrous deep green leaves. This plant makes a good dense hedge.
Culture: It thrives in a mild climate, but will stand some frost and short periods with little water. Near the coast it does well in the open but in hot gardens inland it is advisable to plant it in partial shade.

ACTINIDIA   Chinese Gooseberry, Actinidia
Description: The genus includes twining vines two of which have unusual foliage. The plants are deciduous but the leaves are of some ornamental value for much of the year. Train the plants against a wall, or up a pillar to cover the cross-beams of an arbour or patio, or along a fence to form a screen or hedge. Tie the stems to the support, if necessary, and thin out some of them at the base if growth becomes matted or too exuberant.
Culture: They stand frost but do not flourish in hot dry regions. Where such conditions prevail it is advisable to grow them in partial shade. Plant in soil rich in humus and water them well. They prefer acid to alkaline soil.

A. chinensis   Chinese Gooseberry
The sturdy stems of this Chinese plant have tremendous vitality. They twist and twine about any support available, reaching a height of 10 m, if not headed back. The large leaves are conspicuously ribbed, dark green on the upper surface and pale green on the undersides. All parts of the plant are covered with fine hairs. In summer it bears clusters of lightly fragrant white flowers which turn creamy-yellow as they age. Where cross-fertilisation takes place, these are followed by edible, egg-shaped fruits 4–5 cm long, with a gooseberry flavour. For satisfactory fruiting it is necessary to have male with female plants, or else a plant grafted with both sexes. The cultivar 'Aureo Variegata' which has leaves splashed with cream and yellow, is less vigorous and more suitable for the garden of moderate proportions.

A. kolomikta   Kolomikta Vine
This species, native to Japan, does not range far and wide as does its Chinese relation. It seldom grows to more than 4 m and can therefore be planted in the garden of moderate size. It looks its best trained against a wall. Some of the stems should be cut out when the plant is well grown so that it does not become too bushy. It is grown for its colourful foliage rather than for flowers. Some

46

of the leaves are all white whilst others are green splashed with white, or with pink, white and rose. This delightful colouring of the leaves may not occur during its early years. It has insignificant white flowers in spring followed by small edible but insipid fruits.

ADENOCALYMMA NITIDA

YELLOW TRUMPET

DESCRIPTION: Many beautiful plants – trees, shrubs and climbers – are native to Brazil. This is a twining plant from that country, where it can be found on the fringes of forests, climbing up into the trees. The attractive leathery glossy leaves are oval in form and deep green in colour. In spring, and sometimes during other seasons of the year, it bears clusters of bright canary-yellow flowers consisting of a tube opening to a face made up of unequal segments, rather like those of a bignonia. The flowers are 5–8 cm long and show up well against the dark green of the leaves. Grow it up a pillar or train it over a low table-like support so that one can look down on the foliage and flowers.
CULTURE: This is a plant for humid tropical and subtropical gardens. It can be grown where temperatures occasionally drop to —3°C, but in such regions it should be planted against a wall which will give off some heat at night.

AKEBIA QUINATA   FIVE-LEAF AKEBIA

DESCRIPTION: This evergreen or deciduous climber from Japan and China is a twining plant which grows to 5–6 m or more. Where winters are cold it may prove somewhat slow, but in areas where frosts are not severe it is a quick grower. Its dull maroon flowers which appear in spring have a light fragrance. The leaves are divided into five dark green ovate or obovate leaflets, each one 5–8 cm long and notched at the tip. The purple, rounded fruits are edible but not particularly tasty. It is a climber of some value in a large garden – to cover a tree stump or ugly shed, or to twine about an electric light post. It can also be used as a ground cover to hide a steep dry bank.
CULTURE: Akebia is not very particular as to the soil. If it becomes too rampant in growth, trim it, thinning out some of the stems from the bottom. The plant needs a support about which to twine itself to keep it erect. If cut to the ground by severe cold it usually grows up again quickly in spring. Once established it will survive fairly long periods with little water. It grows in sun and in fairly deep shade.

ALLEMANDA   ALLAMANDA

DESCRIPTION: The genus includes three evergreen plants which are worth growing for their decorative glossy leaves. They have the additional merit of producing very handsome flowers and are therefore deserving of a prominent place in the garden where conditions suit them. Plant them at the bottom of a bank and train them up to hide the bare earth; or tie them against a wall or any other support which will display their beauty to advantage. The main flowering time is spring.
CULTURE: They grow exceptionally well in warm coastal gardens but, given a little protection from drying winds and watered adequately, they will perform well also in inland gardens which do not have more than mild frosts.

A. cathartica   GOLD VINE

In a subtropical garden this one will fling its stems far and wide, but with a little training and tying to a support, and trimming when necessary, it makes an elegant picture. The stems grow to 4 m or more and have almost leathery leaves arranged in whorls. The flower consists of a slender tube opening to a face of wide, recurved segments, measuring as much as 10 cm across. 'Grandiflora' and 'Hendersonii' are two cultivars even better-looking than their parent.

A. neriifolia

This is more of a shrub than a true climber but, if the stems are trained fanwise against a wall it makes a pretty show. The shining leaves form a good foil to the clusters of trumpet-shaped flowers, which are richly coloured golden-yellow with a flush of copper on the outside.

A. violacea

Is not as decorative as the other two species, but worth growing in a warm garden. The leaves, arranged in whorls, show up to advantage its cyclamen-pink flowers. It produces some flowers in winter as well as in spring.

ALOE CILIARIS   CLIMBING ALOE

DESCRIPTION: This dainty aloe is not a true climber but as it looks best when trained against a wall or about the bole of a tree, it is included in this book.

Yellow Trumpet Climber (*Adenocalymma nitida*) does best in warm regions with high humidity.

Actinidia (*A. kolomikta*) is a Chinese plant worth growing for its gaily tinted leaves.

It has typical aloe leaves which are decorative throughout the year, and in winter it puts on a brilliant display. The cylindrical flowerheads are composed of tubular flowers of a rich tomato-red tipped with lime-green. If the plant is not tied to a support it sprawls across the ground in a rather ungainly fashion. Planted among shrubs, it will grow up and through them, bearing its flowers above them. The flowers are useful for arrangements as well as being decorative in the garden. The stems grow to 2–3 m.

CULTURE: This South African plant does well at the coast and also in dry areas and in poor soil. It will tolerate occasional sharp frosts, but is not happy in cold, damp gardens.

AMPELOPSIS BREVIPEDUNCULATA
BLUEBERRY CLIMBER

DESCRIPTION: A rampant climber to 6 m or more, with twining tendrils which enable it to cling to any support. It is a deciduous plant with large handsome leaves. They have three to five lobes and are dark green in colour. The flowers are inconspicuous and the plant is grown for its foliage and the grape-like berries which turn a metallic blue when ripe. This is a useful plant to grow along the boundary of a large property or to provide shade over an arbour or pergola. It is not recommended for the small town garden. 'Elegans' is a fine cultivar which is better suited to the small garden as it is less vigorous in growth. Its leaves are mottled with white and pink. Planted in a container it forms a decorative patio plant.

CULTURE: Grows in sun or shade and stands severe frost. In regions where frosts are mild it may not shed all of its leaves. Mature plants will endure long periods with little water.

ANEMOPAEGMA CHAMBERLAYNII
(*Bignonia chamberlaynii*) YELLOW TRUMPET VINE

DESCRIPTION: There are several most attractive bignonias worth growing for the beauty of their foliage or flowers. This is a rampant evergreen climber from Brazil which supports itself by tendrils. Because of its speedy growth it is a useful climber for covering the netting around a tennis court. The leaves are divided into two leaflets 15 cm long. Clusters of yellow, trumpet-shaped flowers appear in summer. It bears a resemblance to the Cat's Claw Creeper (Doxantha).

CULTURE: Being native to tropical America this

Allemanda (*A. cathartica*) has pleasing foliage and large, handsome flowers.

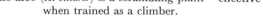
...is little aloe (*A. ciliaris*) is a scrambling plant – effective when trained as a climber.

The graceful sprays of Coral Creeper (*Antigonon leptopus*) lend elegance to the summer garden.

plant is not suitable for very cold gardens, although it will survive occasional sharp frosts. When grown against a trellis or the walls of the house it should be trimmed at least once a year, otherwise it is likely to cover too large an area.

ANTIGONON LEPTOPUS CORAL CREEPER, QUEEN'S WREATH, HONOLULU CREEPER

DESCRIPTION: This is a charming plant with trailing sprays of dainty shrimp-pink flowers tumbling all over the plant in frothy masses in late summer and early autumn. Under optimum conditions it is a rampant grower climbing and twining to as much as 7 m. The attractive heart- or arrow-shaped leaves of mid-green are sparsely carried along the stems, giving the plant a light and airy appearance. In warm districts it is ever-green but in cold areas it loses most of its leaves.

This is a fine plant for growing up the bole of a tall tree where there is sufficient sunshine. It looks most decorative, too, when used as a ground cover, spilling over a bank or wall, or when trained up the walls of a building, or on a trellis over a patio. It also makes a pretty show when trained on a fence. There is a white form but it is not as ornamental as the pink one.

CULTURE: Coral creeper is a decorative, quick-growing, Mexican plant which enjoys warm grow-ing conditions, and, where winter temperatures drop to freezing, it may die down to the ground. This may prove a blessing in the garden of average size as it obviates the necessity of cutting the plant back to keep it under control. As soon as spring comes it rises again and grows with cheerful aban-don. It will not do well in cool, shady gardens, but revels in hot sunny places with high humidity. Where it is not cut back by winter cold, trim it occasionally to keep it within bounds. In gardens which have more than 3° of frost put a thick mulch over the ground to protect the roots. Established plants stand considerable drought.

ARAUJIA SERICOFERA

CRUEL PLANT

DESCRIPTION: This is not a particularly decorative climber but a useful plant for wind-swept gardens and poor soil. Under suitable conditions it is quick and may grow to 4 m in a couple of years. It is an evergreen of twining habit with long leaves, mid-green on the upper surface and pale green on the underside. The faintly-scented flowers of ivory-white, attractive in form but not very showy, are followed by seed capsules 12 cm long containing numerous silky, tufted seeds which are likely to be carried by the wind and appear in other parts of the garden. The common name of Cruel Plant refers to the fact that moths visiting the flowers are often held trapped by their proboscis.
CULTURE: This climber grows best in warm humid regions but once established will tolerate frost and drought. It develops quickly in full sun or in part shade. It is not recommended for small gardens because of its tendency to seed itself freely.

ARISTOLOCHIA   DUTCHMAN'S PIPE

DESCRIPTION: A large genus of plants, some of which are climbers with flowers which are curious rather than pretty. They are of little ornamental value in the small garden but are interesting plants to use for quick cover in a large garden or park. Planted at the base of a tree they will climb up into it.
CULTURE: They do best when grown in areas of high humidity. They are unlikely to thrive where hot, dry winds prevail, or where the air is dry for most months of the year. Plant in good soil in partial or full shade because bright sun tends to make the foliage limp. Water well during dry seasons of the year. If plants become too large cut them back or remove some stems near the base in late winter and early spring. One of the species described is somewhat tender, the other two are frost-resistant.

A. californica   CALIFORNIA DUTCHMAN'S PIPE
A deciduous climber which reaches a height of 3–4 m and has large bright green, heart-shaped leaves. In late winter and early spring before the new leaves appear it produces its unusual flowers which are cream when young, marked with purplish red mottling as they mature. It does best in partial shade and stands severe frost.

A. elegans   DUTCHMAN'S PIPE
A Brazilian species with large heart-shaped leaves and flowers like an old-fashioned curved pipe. The basal curve is yellowish green and the bowl of the 'pipe' is of maroon strangely marked and mottled with ivory. The flowers are much larger than those of the species described above. This species does best where winters are mild and where it has some shade and an abundance of moisture. The flowering time is summer.

A. macrophylla   DUTCHMAN'S PIPE
(A. durior)
This species from the eastern part of the United States does best in cool gardens where it will grow to 6 m in a couple of years. The dark green leaves are heart or kidney-shaped and up to 30 cm long. The curiously formed flowers are curved in the lower part, yellowish green at the base and brownish purple at the end. It should be grown where it is sheltered from bright sun and drying winds and given an abundance of water.

ARRABIDEA   CHERRY VINE

DESCRIPTION: The genus includes two quick-growing climbers and twiners. They are pretty plants for growing over a trellis to provide shade on a pergola or patio, or to attach to a wall to add colour to the house. They are related to the bignonias which have become popular in many countries of the world.
CULTURE: They like warm, humid growing conditions, and are therefore suitable only for tropical and subtropical gardens.

A. mollissima
A handsome and vigorous plant from the Philippines with thick leaves and festoons of pink to cyclamen flowers with a delicate fragrance. Under optimum conditions it may grow too quickly and need cutting back once a year to keep it within bounds.

A. rotundata
Is a rampant climber from Malaysia which bears showers of pink to rose flowers when the leaves

have fallen. The flowers are broadly bell-shaped with a mouth rather like a bignonia.

ASPARAGUS PLUMOSUS
FERN ASPARAGUS, EMERALD FEATHER

DESCRIPTION: Fern asparagus is a delightful evergreen plant for small gardens or for growing in pots indoors or on a shady patio. It reaches a height of 2 m and has delicate, feathery leaves as dainty as fine lace. It is grown for the beauty of its leaves. The tiny white flowers and purple berries are not showy. The foliage is used by florists in all countries of the world for bouquets, and it is well worth growing in the garden to provide material for home arrangements. It should be tied to a stake to keep it erect.
CULTURE: Although this South African plant tolerates moderate frost it should not be exposed to continuous dry cold for long periods. In regions where winters are long and severe, plant it in a container which can be moved indoors during the coldest months. It does well in the open at the coast but needs some shade in inland gardens.

ASTERANTHERA OVATA
DESCRIPTION: From the rain forests of southern Chile comes this plant which climbs up the boles of trees, attaching itself by means of aerial roots. It grows to 3–4 m and is an evergreen with dark green ovate or rounded leaves 1–4 cm long. The flowers are tubular with a star-shaped face of four segments. They are strawberry-red and show up well against the large green calyx. The main flowering time is summer. Plant under trees or use as a shady ground cover.
CULTURE: It needs shade and a cool soil rich in leaf-mould. Severe frost will not affect it but dryness will inhibit growth.

BEAUMONTIA GRANDIFLORA
HERALD'S TRUMPET, EASTER LILY VINE

DESCRIPTION: This Indian plant is one of the most decorative of climbing plants for gardens where winters are mild. It sends up sturdy stems which grow to as much as 6 m in height. The large dark green glossy leaves are very handsome and at certain times of the year they assume lovely yellow and bronze tints. Being evergreen it is decorative throughout the year, and when it flowers in spring it is a magnificent sight. The flowers appear in clusters – each one a huge white trumpet like a lily. They give off a delicate sweet scent, rather like that of gardenia.

Beaumontia is a good climber for a large expanse of wall, to train over a strong trellis or along a fence. It is decorative, too, when cut back to shrub size. In regions where winters are cold grow it as a shrub on a sheltered patio.
CULTURE: If planted against a wall which holds the warmth in winter beaumontia will endure occasional drops in temperature to freezing. It needs good soil and regular watering to keep it flourishing.

BERBERIDOPSIS CORALLINA
CORAL PLANT

DESCRIPTION: This scandent evergreen shrub from Chile can be trained against a wall or fence to act as a climber. Its slender stems grow to 4 m. The ovate- to heart-shaped leaves are thick and leathery, with spines along the margins. In summer the small bright coral-red flowers show up beautifully against the leaves. This is a dainty plant for a cool sheltered patio.
CULTURE: Requires acid or neutral soil with a cool root run and a shady situation. Protect it from hot dry wind and water well during dry periods of the year. It is hardy to frost.

BIGNONIA
TRUMPET VINE AND OTHERS

DESCRIPTION: Botanists have re-classified the plants formerly known as bignonias but many of them are still listed in nursery catalogues under their old names. Because the new names are not universally known, a list of the most popular ones is given below, together with the new names under which they are described in this book.

Bignonia cherere	– see *Phaedranthus buccinatorius*
Bignonia chinensis	– see *Campsis grandiflora*
Bignonia jasminoides	– see *Pandorea jasminoides*
Bignonia magnifica	– see *Saritaea magnifica*
Bignonia purpurea	– see *Clytostoma binatum*
Bignonia radicans	– see *Campsis radicans*
Bignonia speciosa	– see *Clytostoma callistegioides*
Bignonia tweediana	– see *Doxantha unguis-cati*
Bignonia venusta	– see *Pyrostegia venusta*
Bignonia violacea	– see *Clytostoma callistegioides*

Araujia sericofera. Not a showy plant but it grows quickly under adverse conditions.

The flowers of Dutchman's Pipe (*Aristolochia elegans*) are more curious than beautiful.

BIGNONIA CAPREOLATA CROSS VINE

DESCRIPTION: A robust climbing plant native to the south-eastern United States which, under favourable conditions, could become a pest. It is an evergreen or semi-evergreen which climbs by means of leaf tendrils which twine about any support. It will cover a large area of wall or fence or a tree very quickly. The tubular flowers 5 cm long flare out at the ends and are yellow marked with terra-cotta or orange. In full bloom it makes a colourful show. The leaves are ovate and usually arranged in pairs.

CULTURE: In warm humid conditions this plant may prove too vigorous in growth and need frequent trimming to keep it within bounds. Established plants stand moderate to sharp frost, but when damaged by frost, new growth shoots out rapidly again in spring.

BILLARDIERA LONGIFLORA

PURPLE APPLEBERRY

DESCRIPTION: This twining evergreen plant, native to Tasmania, is slender in growth and therefore suitable for small gardens and for growing in containers. It has narrow deep green leaves 2–4 cm long and small tubular creamy flowers in spring which hang down prettily on thin stems emerging from the axils of the leaves. When the flowers fade the plant carries oblong burgundy fruits 2–3 cm long. Plant it against a wall which will show up its graceful form, or let it drape itself over a wall.

CULTURE: It stands severe frost and grows best in part shade. Plant in rich soil and water regularly during long dry periods.

BOMAREA BOMAREA

DESCRIPTION: The genus includes a number of small but handsome twining plants, closely related to alstroemeria, with flowers similar in form and colouring. Some of them have tuberous or fleshy roots, and they have a definite growing season from spring to the end of autumn, followed by a dormant season when the top growth dies down. These are twiners to use in containers to embellish the patio, terrace or house in summer when they flower, and to store out of sight when they are dormant in winter. Provide a light stake for them to twine about.

CULTURE: Bomarea require a humus-rich soil and an abundance of water during the months they

A bougainvillea grown as a standard is elegant and ornamental in any part of the garden.

are in active growth. When they die down, water lightly once a week. They can be grown in regions with cold winters provided the roots are protected from frost by a thick mulch over the ground. At the coast they can be grown in the open but in hot districts inland they do better in open or partial shade.

B. acutifolia

A Mexican plant with slender pointed leaves. The flowers are carried in dainty clusters at the ends of the stems. They are yellow with flecks of rose and crimson.

B. caldasiana

The tubular flowers appear in graceful drooping clusters at the ends of the stems – the main flowering time being late summer and early autumn. They are crimson and yellow, decorative on the plant and in arrangements.

B. edulis

This South American species needs a warm humid climate. The flower segments are rose or yellow tipped and flecked with green. The tubers are said to have been eaten by the Indians in days gone by.

B. kalbreyeri

Grows up quickly in spring and begins to produce its enchanting clusters of flowers by mid-summer. They are funnel-shaped, 2–3 cm long, prettily coloured coral-red outside and orange-yellow spotted with red inside.

B. multiflora

A Venezuelan species which sends up new growth each spring to a height of 2–3 m. It has twining stems sparsely clothed with foliage like that of a lily and bears spectacular clusters of flowers in summer. The flowers are trumpet-shaped and of a rich coral-red liberally spotted with mahogany inside.

BOUGAINVILLEA   BOUGAINVILLEA

DESCRIPTION: No plant produces a more magnificent mantle of colour than the bougainvillea. The flowers themselves are small and inconspicuous but they are surrounded by three brilliantly coloured bracts generally referred to as the flowers. The colours range from palest mauve, through magenta to a rich shade of purple; from white through biscuit-yellow to terra-cotta; and from

This bougainvillea – Mrs. Palmer – with two-tone flowering stems, is a sensational sight.

A double-flowering bougainvillea makes a gay container or background plant for a border.

Plant bougainvillea to camouflage an outbuilding or screen a patio.

pale pinky-rose to glowing wine red. Some of the newest cultivars bear flowers with bracts of different colours on the same plant. The main flowering period is from late spring to late summer, but in warm regions they will produce flowers throughout the year. The leaves are variable in size, generally dark green on the upper surface and paler on the underside, oval and pointed.

These colourful plants can be used in many ways to highlight the garden. They look decorative trained against a wall, along a fence or as a hedge. They can be trimmed to shrub size or trained to form standard plants or small shade trees with drooping stems of flowers, and they can be grown most effectively on an arch or pergola, up into a tree, or as a ground cover. Some of them make a splendid show when grown in containers, and, in areas where winter is severe they should be grown in this way and moved to a warm sheltered part of the garden for the cold months of the year.

B. glabra and *B. spectabilis* are the vigorous and hardy species with magenta bracts from which many named hybrids have been evolved. Amongst the new cultivars are some which have double flowers and some which have variegated leaves. The following are the names of a few good cultivars with double flowers: 'Bridal Bouquet' (pink/cerise/white); 'Golden Doubloon' (yellow/orange/pink); 'Pink Champagne' (magenta/rose); 'Philippine Parade' (rose), and 'Princess Mahara' (ruby-red). Generally these are not as vigorous in growth as the species and older hybrids and therefore more suitable for the garden of moderate dimensions.

CULTURE: Bougainvilleas are sun and heat-loving plants. They grow best under fairly dry conditions and tolerate occasional sharp frost but not prolonged damp cold. They grow remarkably well in many gardens which experience quite severe frost if they are against a north wall which warms up during the day and retains some of the heat at night. In tropical and subtropical regions they grow into large plants very quickly whereas in areas where the temperature frequently drops below freezing they are apt to be cut back, but this can prove a blessing in disguise as otherwise the plants might grow too large. In areas with cold winters set out new plants in spring so that they are well-grown before the next cold season. Should plants appear to be growing too vigorously and producing few flowers cut out some of the long stems and head back laterals fairly hard.

Because bougainvilleas are lusty plants with tremendous vitality they need regular trimming and training to keep them neat and to prevent them from taking over too much of the garden. When the plant is still young it is wise to do this frequently, shortening a surplus stem every two or three weeks, rather than cutting it out at the base at one go and so causing shock to the plant. Old established plants will stand severe pruning without flinching.

With young plants allow the first shoots to grow to about 45 cm and tie them around each other so that they form a wheel close to the ground. As soon as the plants are established they will send up thick vigorous stems ready to be trained in the way they are to grow. Generally plants distributed by nurseries have already reached this stage of growth with one or more main stems or canes coming up from ground level.

If a bougainvillea is to be trained against a wall or fence, retain two main stems and train them parallel to the ground, along the fence or wall. Upright shoots will emerge from these and they should in turn be fastened to the wall as they grow. Watch the tips of the original main stems as they can quickly outgrow their allotted space on the wall unless they are trimmed from time to time.

A hedge can be developed in much the same way. Plant the same variety to make the hedge, setting the plants 2–3 m apart. In this case allow several stems to grow out from the base and fasten them to stakes on either side so that they spread out parallel to the ground, one above the other. Upright shoots will emerge, and when these are about 45 cm long turn them down onto the lower horizontal and tie them in, making a kind of entanglement. As the growth spreads out trim it off along the sides so that the hedge does not become too wide and also to encourage dense growth within the hedge. Established bougainvillea hedges require little trimming, but it must be done regularly, particularly during the warmer months when growth is fast.

Bougainvilleas trained as standards are procurable from nurseries but those who wish to experiment and create their own standards or small trees should follow this method. Procure or make a frame with an umbrella-like top firmly attached to an upright of the required height. See that the whole thing is durable and anchor the upright firmly in the ground so that it will not move during high wind. Plant the bougainvillea in the hole, which should have been prepared beforehand, and tie one of the stems to the up-right in several places. If there are laterals coming out from this main stem below the umbrella-like top, remove them, and continue to remove any which may emerge later. As this stem thickens see that the ties are not too tight and allow some side shoots to develop above the umbrella, but trim them back two or three times a year so that the top-growth is not too heavy for the main stem, and cut out any additional stems which emerge from the base. In time the top-growth will make a small tree-like crown to the thickened stem. (see illustration on page 52)

To cover an arch or arbour it is advisable to allow only one main stem to develop initially, and to remove others near ground level. When the single main stem has grown higher than the upright of the arch, arbour or pergola, bend it gently and tie it to the crossbeam, and, as lateral shoots develop from the section overhead tie them in around the crossbeam. Only when this is properly clothed should additional basal shoots be allowed to develop. One or two of these can then be wound around the upright to hide it from view. Remember, however, to watch for excessive growth and cut it back. This is best done after the flowering is over, but tip pruning can be done at any time.

Bougainvilleas grown in containers are splendid plants to bring forward onto a terrace or patio when they are in full flower. Like other plants in containers they need more regular feeding than those growing in the ground and should receive a potplant fertiliser every month.

When grown as a ground cover bougainvillea stems must be supported above the ground. Make a strong frame about 30–60 cm above ground onto which the developing shoots can be trained. Such a frame may be of wires stretched taut between stakes projecting 30–60 cm above the ground, but a more rigid frame is recommended, using wire mesh attached to a frame of galvanised tubing. A frame for a single plant should be not less than 2 m across – square or round. Bougain-villeas are suitable as ground cover only in large gardens or parks or along highways. The trimming and tying in of developing shoots must be done regularly to keep the cover neat and to discourage unwanted growth. Generally it is advisable to allow only one main stem to develop as this will provide enough laterals to cover the frame.

A bougainvillea flowering at the top of a tree makes an impressive sight and it is not difficult to train a plant up along one main stem to do this. Cut out unnecessary laterals as they develop lower down. If the bougainvillea is not trained to one main stem for at least one-half of the height of the tree it will scramble all over it and hide it from view completely.

Bougainvilleas are useful also for clothing steep banks. If possible plant at the bottom of the bank and encourage one stem to grow up and over the bank by removing additional basal stems. The laterals which develop from the one stem will make a neat cover over the bank.

Where, through neglect, it is necessary to prune a bougainvillea severely, do this if possible after the main flowering season is over.

The following are the names of a few of the many good cultivars available:

'Afterglow'	A profuse bloomer with yellow-orange flowers in large trusses.
'Alba'	Has white bracts. Looks effective when trained up through a tree.
'Apple Blossom'	Also known as 'Jamaica White'. The white bracts are sometimes tinged with pink.
'Barbara Karst'	Stands dry, almost desert-like conditions; is vigorous and bears cerise flowers.
'Beryl Lemmer'	An exquisite white cultivar raised in Rhodesia. It is more tolerant of frost than many others.
'Brilliant'	Buds open copper-red and change to cherry and crimson. Ideal for tub-culture.
'David Lemmer'	Has large blood-red bracts. Grow it as a tree or into a tree.
'Dream'	Also known as 'Moonlight'. Ivory shading to lilac. Vigorous and floriferous.
'Formosa'	Also known as 'Pride of Singapore'. Has flowers shaded from lilac to mauve. Rampant grower and a good one to grow as a tree.

'Gladys Hepburn'	Is a bushy type with glossy leaves and large trusses of carmine pink bracts.
'Indian Flame'	Copper to flaming cerise-red. Makes a brilliant show of colour.
'James Walker'	A free-flowering cultivar of robust growth with large bracts shaded from brick to cerise.
'Jennifer Fernie'	Bears a mass of large white bracts in large trusses on long stems.
'Killie Campbell'	A rampant grower with flowers which change in colour as they mature – from rust to ruby and cyclamen.
'Lady Mary Baring'	Has bracts of ochre to majolica which pale as they age to a softer hue.
'Lemmer's Special'	A floriferous cultivar with fiery copper-red bracts on strong stems.
'Magnifica'	Stands more frost than most bougainvilleas and has glossy foliage. Bright mauve to purple bracts.
'Mary Palmer'	Is an unusual and very lovely one. Bracts of pure white and cyclamen are carried on the same stems.
'McLean'	Is a strong grower with orange flowers in large clusters.
'Millarii'	Also known as 'Golden Glow'. Golden-yellow fading to apricot and pink.
'Mrs. Butt'	An old variety which produces masses of flowers of deep burgundy.
'Orange King'	A sturdy type with long stems of flowers of bronze fading to apricot and later to shrimp-pink.
'Philippine Parade'	A new cultivar with huge heads of double flowers of candy-pink, fading to rose as they age.
'Poulton's Special'	A strong grower and free-flowering type with large bracts of deep rose fading to maroon.
'Princess Mahara'	Has dense clusters of flowers made up of double bracts of brilliant cerise to ruby-red.
'Scarlet O'Hara'	One of the hardiest and one of the most vigorous, with attractive foliage and brilliant red bracts.
'Texas Dawn'	Bears cerise to cyclamen bracts on plants of moderate growth.

CALONYCTION ACULEATUM
(*Ipomoea bona-nox*)   SCENTED MOON VINE,
MOONLIGHT CONVOLVULUS

DESCRIPTION: A delightful climber with flowers of ethereal loveliness, which open only at night and during the summer months. It should therefore be sited in a part of the garden where one is likely to sit in the evening, or near a window so that its sweet gardenia-like perfume can pervade the house. On a warm evening one can actually see the quivering movement of the flower buds as they unfurl. This may take as little as five minutes or as long as half-an-hour, depending on weather.

This twining plant has many attributes. It is very quick-growing and, in a subtropical garden, may develop from seed to flowering in three months. The large, soft, heart-shaped leaves are decorative and the stems twine themselves gracefully about any support and move rapidly up to roof level. Each flower consists of a long ice-green tube which opens to a luminous white, trumpet-shaped face 10–12 cm across. Delicate wedge-shaped markings of palest green run from circumference to centre. Until the buds unfurl there is no scent but, as the flowers open, it seems to burst forth as though to summon with the utmost immediacy the night insects which must pollinate it. In the morning as the sun rises the flowers fold up, and by the time the light is intense, they are closed, never to open again. However, a single

Bougainvilleas are splendid climbers for adding colour and beauty for many months of the year. (Brilliant)

The enchanting flowers of the Moonlight Convolvulus (Calonyction) scent the garden from dusk to dawn.

plant will bear many hundreds of buds, and each night, for two or three months, one can enjoy this dramatic and lovely spectacle. Picked in the late afternoon the flowers can be used for a superlative dinner-table arrangement, as they open indoors at night, on the night they are picked.

CULTURE: In a tropical or subtropical garden the plant should be trimmed back to keep it from spreading too far and wide. It has a tendency also to root along the ground. Such offshoots are easily removed when young. If allowed to develop they will cover neighbouring plants very quickly. It stands moderate frost and fairly long periods of drought. In cold gardens it can be grown also as an annual. Small plants set out in spring will start flowering by the beginning of summer. It can be grown from seed too. Put the seeds in warm water and allow them to soak for several hours to promote rapid germination.

CAMPSIS TRUMPET CREEPER, BIGNONIA

DESCRIPTION: This genus includes three deciduous climbers which are vigorous in habit and have attractive foliage and large handsome trumpet-shaped flowers. They can be grown along walls and fences or allowed to cascade down over a bank, trained over a trellis or arch, or against the walls of the house.

CULTURE: Trumpet creepers endure cold weather and they will also grow well in regions with a low rainfall and hot summers.

C. grandiflora CHINESE TRUMPET CREEPER
(*Bignonia chinensis*)

A vigorous climber to 6 m with pretty flowers measuring 7 cm in length, varying in colour from apricot to red. The flower consists of a trumpet with a face of five uneven lobes. They are carried in large showy clusters in summer. The leaves are divided into seven or nine oval leaflets with deeply and irregularly toothed margins.

C. radicans COMMON TRUMPET CREEPER
(*Bignonia radicans*)

This native to the eastern United States stands freezing conditions. If the top growth is frosted off, the plant grows up rapidly again. It will cover a fence to 9 m in a couple of years. The leaves are divided into ovate leaflets with toothed margins. The showy clusters of terra-cotta flowers which appear in summer are similar to those of *C. grandiflora* but they are more tubular and narrower at the mouth. Because of its habit of suckering, it is not recommended for gardens of moderate size but could be used effectively on dry banks along a road or drive, or to form the boundary to a large property. It clings to a support by means of small rootlets on the stems. 'Flava' is a pretty cultivar with rich yellow flowers.

C. x tagliabuana

This is a hybrid of the two species described above. A cultivar of this, known as 'Madame Galen' has become very popular in gardens in many countries. It is suitable for gardens large and small. The handsome large salmon-red flowers make a really splendid show in summer. This plant looks effective trained up around a pillar or over a trellis, or treated as a shrub. Young plants need some support but after a few years the main stem becomes strong enough to support the plant.

CEANOTHUS CALIFORNIAN LILAC

DESCRIPTION: Ceanothus include deciduous and evergreen shrubs, most of which are native to California. They vary considerably in size and some of the cultivars make a splendid show when trained to grow flat against a wall like a climber. The main flowering time is spring. The fact that they bear blue flowers is an additional attribute as there are not many plants with flowers of this colour. The colour varies from palest powder blue to a rich cobalt. The individual flowers are tiny but they are carried in densely packed little spikes which show up well against the background of dark green leaves. Two of the best of the species from which many hybrids have developed are *C. papillosus* and *C. thyrsiflorus*. The following are the names of some good cultivars: 'A. T. Johnson', 'Autumnal Blue', 'Delight', and 'Italian Skies'. All of them are evergreen.

CULTURE: These plants do well in cool regions and once they are established they will also endure drought, but to ensure good flowering it is advisable to water them in winter when bud development begins. To keep them neat train some of the stems against a wall, tying them firmly to the wall in a fanlike fashion. When too many stems emerge from the base, as will happen in time, cut these off. The stems trained against the wall will also, with the passing of years, become too exuberant in growth. When this happens trim or cut back the stems immediately after the flowering period is over. Ceanothus will grow in acid or slightly alkaline soil, inland and at the coast. They are not recommended for subtropical gardens, but do well in regions where strong winds may be a problem.

CELASTRUS CELASTRUS

DESCRIPTION: A genus of 30 species some of which are shrubs and some twiners. The latter require some form of support when grown against a wall but will embrace a pillar or scramble over a bank with little encouragement. These are useful plants in the large garden or park – for clothing large expanses of wall, tall fences, tree stumps or arbours. The small flowers which appear in summer are insignificant. The plants are grown for the small brightly coloured fruits which follow in autumn and winter. In some species the flowers are unisexual and, to ensure the production of fruits, both male and female plants should be grown.

CULTURE: They endure severe frost and grow in full sun or shade. Mature plants tolerate long periods with little water.

C. hypoleucus

A rampant climber to 9 m having leaves which are glaucous on the underside and young shoots covered with a purplish bloom. The fruiting capsules are lined with yellow and open to display scarlet seeds.

The shrubby ceanothus makes a striking picture if trimmed and trained against a wall.

C. orbiculatus
(*C. articulatus*)

This vigorous species reaching up to 12 m is bisexual and single plants will fruit. The leaves may turn yellow in autumn. At this time also the brown seed capsules open to reveal their yellow lining and crimson seeds, which make a delightful show.

CHONEMORPHA MACROPHYLLA
(*Trachelospermum fragrans*)   MALAYAN JASMINE

DESCRIPTION: A rampant climber native to Malaysia where it forms stout lianas in the forests, reaching to the tops of the tallest trees. The leaves of the plant are large and lush, up to 30 cm long and half this in width, ovate to oval in form. The creamy-white flowers appear in summer and scent the air with a jasmine-like fragrance. Each flower is made up of a short tube which flares into 5 segments arranged obliquely – somewhat like the blades of a ship's propeller. They are about 10 cm in diameter.

CULTURE: This is a plant for the tropical garden where humidity is high and where the soil is rich in humus. Grow it in partial shade and once it is established, trim it back hard once a year to keep it from ranging too far afield.

CISSUS   KANGAROO VINE

DESCRIPTION: The genus includes a diversity of plant forms, amongst which are four evergreen climbers cultivated for their handsome foliage. They are quick-growing in the garden but remain small and of ornamental value when growing in containers to grace the house, terrace, courtyard or patio. They have strong tendrils which will attach the plant to any support provided – be it a small cane in a pot, or a post or pillar in the garden. If grown indoors stand the container in a position where there is good light.

CULTURE: They do best in regions with a mild climate, and are not suitable for gardens where winters are severe but they may be grown successfully in containers which can be moved under cover during winter. Where winters are not extreme the eaves of the house and a south-facing wall will provide enough shelter for most of them. They do best in partial shade.

C. antarctica   KANGAROO VINE
An Australian species which has been popular for many years. In the garden it may grow to 6 m but in a pot it seldom reaches more than 2 m. Its shiny dark green leaves are broadly ovate with toothed edges. It is a good container plant indoors or out-of-doors, and can be trained to grow up a support and trimmed to shape, or allowed to cascade over a bank or wall.

C. discolor
A decorative foliage plant from India which under suitable garden conditions may reach a height of 6 m. As a container plant indoors where its beautiful leaves can be appreciated to the full it seldom reaches more than 1–2 m. It is a tropical plant needing both heat and humidity. Cold and dry winds destroy the foliage. The leaves are broadly ovate and up to 15 cm long, of vivid green richly veined with white and purple on the upper surface and crimson on the underside. Train the stems up a support or plant it in a hanging basket and let them tumble down over the edges.

C. hypoglauca
A rampant Australian species reaching 3 m in a year, eventually growing to 9 m, if not cut back. The glossy leaves are divided into five rounded leathery leaflets 6 cm long. The new growth is covered with rusty-coloured silky hairs. Train it up a fence or over pillars or let it tumble down to hide the bare earth on a bank.

C. rhombifolia   GRAPE IVY
This species from South America grows to 6 m out-of-doors but it is usually raised as an indoor plant. The beautiful deep green foliage consists of diamond-shaped leaflets with toothed edges. The new growth is covered with bronze hairs. It grows in sun or fairly deep shade and can be used under trees. It stands only mild frost.

C. striata
A luxuriant climber with leaves made up of five obovate dark green glossy leaflets with toothed edges. It bears a resemblance to the popular Virginia creeper. It grows to 3 m and looks effective against a wall, spilling over a bank, or as ground cover. Stands sun or shade and moderate frost.

CLEMATIS   CLEMATIS

DESCRIPTION: More than two hundred names of clematis species and hybrids are recorded. Most of them are deciduous climbing plants with attractive flowers followed by seedheads which are also decorative. Clematis include some of the most beautiful of all the climbing plants for gardens where winters are cold. There are species and hybrids suitable for the small garden as well as the large one, where space is not a limiting factor. Clematis are decorative when trained against a wall, up a trellis, over an arch, about a dead tree stump, up into a living tree or along a fence. Their flowers are delightful in arrangements, too. The flower is composed of four to eight sepals – usually large and colourful, sometimes referred to as tepals. The fluffy seedheads decorate the plants for many weeks after the flowers have faded. They, too, look effective in arrangements. Some of the species are vigorous in growth but many of the cultivars remain small and they are therefore excellent plants for small gardens. They cling to any support provided, or to neighbouring plants, by their twining leaf stalks.

CULTURE: For good results plant them in rich soil to which 2–3 handfuls of bonemeal have been added, in a position where the ground round about the roots is shaded from the sun. Some authorities assert that they need alkaline soil for their best development, whilst others believe that they do just as well in acid soil. The tops of the plants will flourish in sunlight, but in a hot climate where the sunlight is brilliant for much of the year, they should be planted in dappled shade, under a tree with sparse foliage or on the south side of the house. Should it be impractical to have other plants shading the ground, put down a thick mulch of straw or lay flat stones over the soil around the roots. In winter the stems of clematis may appear to be split and dead. They are very brittle and easily broken. Because of this, it is advisable to put in a support when planting, and to tie the plant to the support as the stems grow. Where children or animals are likely to cause damage, protect the stems further with wire-netting. Clematis can stand very cold weather but not long periods of dryness or hot humid conditions. Water them regularly, and particularly well during the growing period, and add fertiliser and compost to the soil every year.

Clematis can be happily grown with other climbers which are not too rampant, using the same support. For example, a late-flowering clematis could share a pillar with a climbing rose, as it would produce its flowers when the rose was past its best.

They are not prone to disease except mildew which is easily kept in check with karathane or any other suitable fungicide, and wilt, for which there is at present no remedy. To reduce the possibility of wilt attacking the plants it is advisable to spray all clematis with a copper-containing fungicide such as bordeaux mixture, in autumn and spring. Two or three applications should be given at fortnightly intervals, covering the ground at the base of the plant as well as its leaves and stems. Another rare disease is caused by a virus which leads to distortion of the flowers. Affected plants should be dug up and burned as they cannot be cured.

C. armandii

This is an evergreen clematis native to China, which grows rapidly to 4 m and bears clusters of glistening white star-shaped flowers in spring, each one 5 cm across. The leaves are composed of three glossy leathery deep green leaflets. It is a robust plant for boundary planting or for growing over a large bank or up a tree. If it needs trimming to keep it within bounds, do this after flowering. Thin out some of the stems near the base and tip-prune others to keep the plant tidy. A cultivar of merit known as 'Apple Blossom' is smaller in habit and has white sepals shaded with pink.

C. brachiata   TRAVELLER'S JOY

A South African species with scented flowers. The leaves are divided and sharply indented and are in themselves of some ornamental value. In summer the flowers composed of four pointed sepals with a crown of golden stamens embellishing the centre add to its appeal. The plant grows to 4–6 m and attaches itself to any support it finds by twining the leaf stems around the support. It is fairly quick-growing. Not recommended for cold gardens.

C. chrysocoma

A beautiful deciduous species from western China growing to about 3 m. It is rather like *C. montana* but is less vigorous and has saucer-shaped white flowers shaded with pink. The flowering time is late spring. Let it make its way up into a tree or drape itself over an arch or out-building.

C. dioscoreifolia   AUTUMN CLEMATIS
(*C. paniculata*)

A vigorous plant, native to Japan, which produces small fragrant creamy white flowers in great abundance in late summer and early autumn. The

Clematis paniculata. An evergreen one which produces a glorious canopy of flowers.

deep green leaves are divided into three to five glossy oval leaflets. Prune hard after flowering.

C. fargesii souliei
A variety of robust growth to 6 m with rather large compound leaves divided into several ovate leaflets. It is a deciduous plant and bears its flowers, with six white petal-like sepals, later in the season than most of the other clematis grown in gardens. They are 4–5 cm across, and appear in late spring and summer.

C. flammula
Grows to 3 m and produces a mass of stems covered with bright green leaves composed of three to five ovate leaflets which show up the myriads of almond-scented white flowers which appear in summer. It is deciduous.

C. x jackmanii
A large-flowered hybrid which reaches a height of 3–4 m and makes a spectacular show in spring and early summer when it flowers. Each flower is 10—12 cm across and has rich violet sepals. Prune hard when necessary in late winter. Many of the large-flowered cultivars now so popular have been bred from this one.

C. lanuginosa
This species from China is the parent of many of the most beautiful of the hybrids grown in gardens to-day. It grows to 2–3 m and bears large flowers measuring 10 cm across. They are white to lilac in colour and appear in mid- to late spring.

C. macropetala
A deciduous species from China with pretty leaves. They are divided into toothed leaflets 2–3 cm long. The flowers of lavender-blue or lilac are composed of sepals within sepals which make them look like double flowers. They hang down gracefully on the plant and, when they fade, their silky seedheads are attractive for a long time. It grows to 2–3 m.

C. montana   ANEMONE CLEMATIS
This clematis is very vigorous in growth and does exceptionally well in cold, damp places. It grows to 8 m or more, and in spring bears masses of white anemone-like flowers about 5 cm across. To keep it within bounds and to encourage good flowering, prune lightly after flowering. 'Rubens' and 'Tetrarose' are the names of two pretty

Clematis 'Lasurstern'. Is a large-flowering hybrid of restrained growth with huge flowers.

hybrids developed from this one. They both have pink to rose-coloured flowers. They are all excellent for growing in trees, over walls or pergolas, as a screen or over outbuildings.

C. paniculata
(*C. indivisa*)
An evergreen species from New Zealand which has variable leaves. It grows to 3–4 m and in spring when it becomes spangled with starry white flowers with golden anthers, it is a really gorgeous sight.

C. tangutica
A native of China which grows to 3–4 m and has grey-green foliage and lovely little yellow, scented, bell-shaped flowers which hang down in clusters. The seedheads which follow are most decorative. The flowering time is summer. It is a good species for fences and trellises, and for covering banks. Prune fairly hard in winter.

C. viticella
A slender climber native to South-east Europe, growing to 3 m. It has pinnate leaves and brick-red to maroon flowers in summer. Prune hard in late winter.

LARGE-FLOWERED GARDEN CLEMATIS
These are derived by hybridisation from various species and they can be numbered as amongst the most spectacular of all garden plants. They do not grow tall, seldom more than 2–3 m, and they are therefore ideal for small gardens. The flowers are glorious and may measure as much as 20 cm across. Plant them where the ground about their roots is shaded, and in hot inland gardens find a position for them where they are not subjected to full sun all day. They do well with only a little morning sun or in open shade all day. They need rich soil and should be given a little fertiliser two or three times a year during their growing season, and compost or well-rotted manure should be lightly forked into the soil once a year. The stems of many of them are very brittle and great care should be taken to ensure that they are not broken when fertilising or at any other time. Water liberally throughout the year.

They need some kind of support about which they can twine their leafstalks. A neat round or square of netting set in a rigid frame mounted on a post one metre above the ground is a good type

Clematis 'Nelly Moser' is one of the most popular of the large-flowering hybrids.

Clematis 'Jackmanii Superba' bears a profusion of flowers of cardinal purple in late spring.

Clematis 'Henryi' has flowers of ethereal loveliness measuring 20 cm across.

of support, for the plant can then spread itself horizontally below eye-level and the beautiful flowers can be seen from above. They also look delightful pushing their way up and through surrounding shrubs. It is important, however, that the shrubs should not have invasive roots which would use up the food and water required by the clematis.

PRUNING: A certain amount of pruning is desirable but not essential. The following suggestions are given to serve as a guide:
1. Those that flower early – that is early to mid-spring – may be trimmed lightly immediately after flowering, by snipping off the flowering stems or seedheads. The letters AF (After Flowering) indicate cultivars best trimmed in this way when flowering is over.
2. Those which flower on the current year's shoots – in late spring or summer, may be pruned hard, to within 60 cm of the ground in winter. The letter w (Winter) indicates cultivars which should be cut back in winter.

'Barbara Jackman'	Has large flowers of lavender-blue with a shimmering flush of claret at the centre of each sepal. AF
'Beauty of Worcester'	A lovely one with violet flowers which are beautifully ornamented by ivory-white stamens. AF
'Belle of Woking'	Bears double flowers of pale mauve early in spring on plants 2 m high. AF
'Blue Gem'	Large lavender-blue flowers with dark stamens in spring. AF
'Comtesse de Bouchaud'	Produces large blush-pink flowers with yellow stamens in late spring. W
'Daniel Deronda'	Large violet-blue flowers with ivory stamens which show up well. AF
'Duchess of Edinburgh'	Double white flowers in spring and occasionally a few in summer. AF
'Duchess of Sutherland'	Burgundy with a dark stripe down the sepals. Flowers sometimes double. AF
'Gipsy Queen'	A vigorous plant with velvety violet sepals and a dark centre. Grow it against a background of shrubs with pale foliage. W
'Hagley Hybrid'	A charming one of delicate rose-pink with cinnamon anthers. Grows to only 2 m. W
'Henryi'	Has glorious huge glistening white flowers with pearl-grey anthers. AF
'Jackmanii Superba'	Large flowers of cardinal purple; a vigorous, free-flowering cultivar. W
'King George V'	Light pink with a deep pink stripe down the centre of the sepals. AF
'Lady Betty Balfour'	Vigorous cultivar with rich purple flowers with gold stamens. W
'Lasurstern'	Large and beautiful purple-blue flowers with striking cream stamens. AF
'Madame Edouard André'	Flowers of rich velvety crimson 15 cm across, with yellow stamens. W
'Marie Boisselot'	Vigorous and free flowering with large impressive white flowers, and yellow stamens. AF
'Mrs. Cholmondeley'	(Pronounced Chumley). A robust cultivar with huge lavender-blue flowers with long pointed sepals. AF
'Nelly Moser'	A popular and lovely cultivar with large flowers of silvery pink with a carmine flush down the centre of each sepal. AF
'Perle d'Azur'	Vigorous with large light lavender-blue flowers and ice-green stamens. W
'The President'	Deep violet with silver on the reverse. Handsome and free-flowering. AF

'Ville de Lyon'	Bright carmine with golden stamens. Very free flowering.
	W
'Vyvian Pennell'	Double flowers of lilac-blue flushed with carmine, are carried on vigorous plants.
	AF
'W. E. Gladstone'	Vigorous and prolific. The large, 20 cm wide flowers of silvery-lavender have purple anthers. AF
'William Kennett'	Bears large deep lavender flowers with amethyst stamens on plants 3 m tall.
	AF

CLERODENDRUM   CLERODENDRON, BLEEDING HEART

DESCRIPTION: The genus includes both shrubs and climbers of merit. The two climbers worth trying are both native to tropical Africa. They differ considerably in habit and flowering.

CULTURE: They do best under warm humid conditions, but once established *C. splendens* will stand cool winters but not much frost. Plant in good soil and water well to promote fast growth. Both species will grow in partial shade provided there is adequate warmth.

C. splendens   CLERODENDRUM

Grows to 9 m in a warm climate but may remain smaller than this in regions where winters tend to be cold. It is a good-looking plant to train up a wall, around a pillar, along a fence or to have trailing over a bank. The broad dark green leaves are more or less heart-shaped at the base, up to 12 cm long and have a wrinkled surface. The tubular, crimson flowers are carried in spectacular clusters mainly in spring, but the plant bears flowers at other seasons too. If the plant grows too large head back some of the new stems and remove a few of the older ones at the base. Does well in part shade.

C. thomsonae   BLEEDING HEART

Under tropical conditions this species may grow to 4 m or more in height. In gardens, where the warmth and humidity are not sufficient to promote growth, it may remain shrub-size. Either way it is a decorative plant. The leaves are up to 12 cm long and shiny. The showy flowers, are made up of a pure white lantern-shaped calyx and a scarlet tubular corolla. They appear in striking clusters in summer. It makes a fine pot plant on a warm patio or courtyard, and is decorative also when grown against a wall or on a trellis. This species prefers shade.

CLIANTHUS PUNICEUS   RED KOWHAI, PARROT'S BEAK

DESCRIPTION: An evergreen scandent shrub with a luxuriant mass of graceful feathery leaves composed of numerous small leaflets. It reaches a height of 3-4 m and bears pendulous clusters of ruby-red, pea-like flowers. Each flower has a long curved keel, which accounts for the common name of Parrot's Beak. The flowers make an opulent show in spring or early summer and are followed by pods 7 cm long. Train the plant against a trellis or along a wall so that the leaves and flowers can be clearly seen. Thin out unwanted growth from the base otherwise the plant will become broad and bushy.

CULTURE: This pretty New Zealand plant can stand considerable frost but it likes to be kept damp. It needs good soil and in hot dry districts it should be planted where it is shaded for much of the day.

CLITORIA TERNATEA   BLUE PEA VINE

DESCRIPTION: An evergreen Indian plant which has to be tied to a support to keep it erect. In a warm climate it reaches 6 m and looks decorative tumbling over a fence or trained up a pillar or against a wall. The leaves are divided into five to nine leaflets of mid-green. The flowers usually appear singly in the leaf axils. They are not showy but very pretty – shaped like those of a pea, mainly blue to amethyst in colour with standard petals beautifully etched with lighter shades. After the flowers fade the plant becomes festooned with slender bean-like pods.

CULTURE: A climber which grows happily in gardens where winters are mild. At the coast it does well in full sun but in hot inland gardens it does best in part shade.

CLYTOSTOMA   PURPLE BIGNONIA, ORCHID TRUMPET VINE

DESCRIPTION: To this genus belong two exceptionally attractive twining plants worth growing in all gardens where conditions suit them. They were once known as bignonias, and both of them have flowers with the characteristic shape of bignonia flowers – i.e. trumpets with a flaring mouth of unequal segments.

CULTURE: They are quick-growing plants which will endure considerable cold and also long periods of drought, when once established. Plant them in good soil to encourage speedy development. They will grow in full sun or partial shade. Trim plants when necessary after flowering to prevent tangling.

C. binatum — PURPLE BIGNONIA
(*Bignonia purpurea*)

A mature plant puts on a most impressive show in spring when it produces its glorious curtains of mauve flowers, beautifully marked in the throat with stripes of a deeper hue. It is an evergreen with pretty lustrous leaves up to 7 cm long which look cheerful throughout the year. The plant is furnished with delicate but strong tendrils which help it to cling to any support. Grow it along a fence to form a hedge or let it drape itself over a pergola or ornament a tree. This species grows to 6 m and stands moderate frost once it is established.

C. callistegioides — ORCHID TRUMPET VINE
(*Bignonia violacea, B. speciosa*)

The manner of growth is very similar to the species described above. It is more vigorous in habit, growing to 9 m, and also more hardy to frost. It is one of the few evergreen climbers which will survive severe cold. The leaves, divided into glossy, dark green leaflets, make a good background throughout the year, and in spring and early summer it bears a mass of orchid-pink to lilac flowers which show up beautifully against the dark green of the leaves. Grow it up a wall, along a fence, on a pergola or over a bank.

COBAEA SCANDENS — CATHEDRAL BELL, CUP-AND-SAUCER VINE

DESCRIPTION: A quick-growing Mexican climber reaching 6 m under suitable conditions. This

Clerodendrum splendens. A climber of great vigour recommended for the large garden.

Bleeding Heart (*Clerodendrum thomsonae*) is restrained in growth and suitable for the patio.

Clianthus puniceus – an evergreen scandent shrub which looks ornamental when trained as a climber.

plant should not be regarded as a perennial for it seldom flowers well after the second or third year. It grows rapidly from seed and produces its unusual flowers within four months of seed-sowing. The flowers are green at first, they then turn mauve and finally violet, and the plant, when in full flower, carries numerous flowers of these three colours. After the flowers fall, the pale green calyces remain decorative for a long time. They are useful for flower arrangements. Its common names aptly describe the flower, for they do indeed look like cathedral bells, and the calyx lies, like a saucer, below the cup-shaped corolla. The leaves are divided into pairs of leaflets with curling tendrils which help the plant to support itself.

CULTURE: As the seeds have a hard coat it is advisable to put them in warm water and allow them to soak for a couple of days before sowing, or else to notch them with a knife. Sow the seed when the weather is warm in spring or start the plants in pots indoors. Cobaea does best in full sunshine, but will grow in filtered shade, too.

COMBRETUM MICROPHYLLUM
BURNING BUSH, FLAME OF THE FOREST

DESCRIPTION: A scandent deciduous shrub from southern Africa, of exuberant growth, recommended for the large garden rather than the small, as it needs a lot of space for its powerful limbs. Unless trimmed to shape, it sends out a mass of whip-like stems. Plant it to fill up space between slow-growing plants, or train the stems against a wall or up over a dead tree trunk. The oval leaves are large, shiny and of a rich green shade which shows up to perfection the clusters of cardinal-red flowers which appear from mid-winter to summer. The flowers are carried in such profusion that the plant from a distance may give the impression of being wreathed in flames, which accounts for the common names of Burning Bush and Flame of the Forest. After the flowers fade its ice-green seedheads remain ornamental for a long time. Other handsome species from tropical

Orchid Trumpet Vine (*Clytostoma callistegioides*) has glorious flowers and pretty foliage.

Cobaea or Cathedral Bell grows quickly from seed sown in spring, to flower by summer.

Flame of the Forest (*Combretum microphyllum*), a robust plant with gay flowers and decorative seeds.

Africa are *C. paniculatum* and *C. platypterium*.
CULTURE: Once established it will stand long periods of drought but not severe frost. Mild frost may cut back some of the shoots but new ones emerge rapidly in spring to flower by summer. Restrain its growth by cutting out one or two stems near the base every year or two, and shortening the others.

CONGEA TOMENTOSA LAVENDER WREATH
DESCRIPTION: A deciduous climber from warm regions of the East, Pakistan to Burma. It tends to be rampant in growth and will quickly cover a large wall or fence. The ovate leaves are heart-shaped at the base, up to 15 cm long, and hairy on the underside. The small white flowers are not showy but they are enclosed by large ornamental bracts ranging in colour from mauve to a dusty purple – and these highlight the plant for some weeks after the flowers have faded. The flowering time is winter and early spring. The stems last well in arrangements when fresh, and they are also useful for dried arrangements.
CULTURE: The plant tolerates some frost but does best in warm regions with high humidity.

CRYPTOSTEGIA GRANDIFLORA
INDIA RUBBER VINE
DESCRIPTION: Although this plant is native to tropical Africa it is referred to as the India rubber vine as it was cultivated in that country for its thick latex from which a kind of rubber is made. This is a scandent evergreen shrub rather than a true climber but the twining stems make it a useful plant to have against a wall or along a fence. The leathery, dark green glossy leaves are 6–10 cm long. Its funnel-shaped flowers somewhat resemble those of allemanda, but they are of a lavender-blue colour. When the flowers fade the plant bears curious angular seedpods, arranged in pairs, like the horns of an ox.
CULTURE: It prefers warm growing conditions, but will grow in regions which experience moderate frost provided the plants are protected for the first three to four years. It does well in coastal gardens.

DENDROMECON RIGIDA BUSH POPPY
DESCRIPTION: This is a shrub rather than a true climber, but, like a few other shrubs, such as

plumbago, it can be trained and trimmed to look effective against the walls of a house or on a trellis. The stems are somewhat rigid when mature and it is therefore advisable to tie the new growth to its support as it elongates. Cut out stems which bush out too much. It is an evergreen with thick narrow leaves up to 10 cm long and bright gold poppy-like, four-petalled flowers in late winter and early spring. The plant is unlikely to grow to more than 2–3 m.
CULTURE: Once established it grows well in dry places and will survive severe frost if protected by a wall.

DIPLADENIA SPLENDENS DIPLADENIA
(*Mandevilla splendens*)
DESCRIPTION: Is a choice evergreen climber of restrained growth. Under optimum conditions it will reach, if supported, a height of 4 m. The twining stems bear oval leaves of mid-green, 10–20 cm long. In spring and summer, when it flowers, it is a most rewarding sight. The elegant flowers appear in clusters about 20 cm across. They are funnel-like with an open face of five rose-pink segments. Plant it against a wall or twine it up around a pillar.
CULTURE: Dipladenia needs good soil and an abundance of water during the dry months. It is native to Brazil and does best in warm humid gardens. Elsewhere, grow it in a pot in a sheltered but airy corner and bring it onto the terrace or patio only when it flowers. In hot inland gardens, where the air is dry, grow it in partial shade and water well, as it likes humidity in the air as well as in the soil. A thick mulch covering the roots will help to retain soil moisture and mitigate frost damage, too.

DIPOGON LIGNOSUS
(*Dolichos gibbosus*) AUSTRALIAN PEA VINE,
ERTJIEBOS
DESCRIPTION: A quick-growing twiner of slender habit which is usually regarded as an annual and grown for temporary cover. It has been given the common name of Australian Pea Vine because it can be found growing wild in some of the hot, dry parts of that continent, where it has naturalized itself, but it is in fact native to South Africa. The leaves are wedge-shaped and about 4 cm across at the base. In summer and early autumn it carries pretty spikes of dainty pea-like flowers. In

South Africa the colour is purple, but those in Australia bear flowers varying in colour from pink through cyclamen to mauve and purple. The pods which follow are rather like those of a pea.

CULTURE: This plant can be grown in any part of the country. Where late frosts occur sow seed after frosts are over. In warm regions seed may be sown in autumn or spring. The plants stand heat and intense sunlight and flower in 3–4 months from seed.

DISTICTIS   VANILLA TRUMPET VINE

DESCRIPTION: Two handsome evergreen climbing plants native to Mexico are included under this name. They climb by means of tendrils to 6 m or more and bear lovely trumpet-shaped flowers.

CULTURE: Like many other plants which come from Mexico they tolerate a wide diversity of climatic conditions. They grow in full sun and in part shade and they do quite well in dry places. Once established they endure severe frost but they do best in regions where winters are not extreme. Be ready to cut off excessive growth as, where conditions suit them, they may romp right through the garden or over the house. Trim them after their flowering time.

D. laxiflora   VANILLA TRUMPET VINE

Has deep green leaflets about 5 cm in length which make a good screen throughout the year. During the warm months the plant becomes covered with clusters of large vanilla-scented flowers. These are violet in colour when they open but fade to lavender as they age. The foliage is lighter green and less lustrous than that of the species described below, and the plant is not as rampant in growth.

D. riversii   ROYAL TRUMPET VINE

A handsome vigorous climber which deserves to be better known and more widely grown. Its mass of shiny leaves is decorative throughout the year and in spring and early summer it bears large clusters of flowers having a cream tube with a face which opens a deep mauve, and fades to a lovely shade of lilac. They appear at the same time as those of *Phaedranthus buccinatorius* (Blood Trumpet) and the two make a splendid show growing together. Prune back when the plant grows too large for its allotted space. It has strong adhesive discs at the ends of tendrils, which enable it to adhere firmly to a support.

DOXANTHA UNGUIS-CATI

(*Bignonia tweediana*)   CAT'S CLAW CREEPER

DESCRIPTION: Is evergreen in warm climates but loses its leaves where winters are cold. This is a vigorous climber which clings to any handy support – wall, fence or trees – by means of strong tendrils which are forked into three parts like the claws of a cat, which accounts for its common name. It reaches a height of 8 m or more. When well grown its curtains of large gold, trumpet-shaped flowers make a splendid display for three to four weeks during late spring and early summer. Each flower is 5–8 cm in length. They have a faint pleasing scent. The leaves are decorative for most of the year and particularly in spring, when the new ones which emerge are tinged with bronze. It is a useful plant for clothing a boundary fence, or to have growing up into a tree or over a dry bank.

CULTURE: Cat's Claw Creeper seems to do best in a sunny situation. It stands quite severe frost and thrives at the coast or in dry places inland. Every year or two some stems should be shortened or cut out at the base to restrict its exuberant growth and to encourage new shoots from the ground.

DREGEA SINENSIS   DREGEA

(*Wattakaka sinensis*)

DESCRIPTION: A deciduous twining plant from China with slender stems which grow to 3 m and need a support. It is a good plant for the small garden or for growing on a terrace where space is limited. The broadly ovate leaves are mid-green on the upper surface and grey on the underside. In summer it bears round clusters of sweetly-scented flowers which have a resemblance to those of the hoya. Each flower consists of a slender tube opening to a starry face. They are white with red dots in the central part.

CULTURE: Once established this dainty plant will stand sharp frost. Where severe frosts are usual, plant it against a north-facing wall, and put a thick mulch of straw over the ground in winter to protect the roots and lower part of the stems. It needs regular watering during dry periods of the year.

ECCREMOCARPUS SCABER

     CHILEAN GLORY FLOWER

DESCRIPTION: This quick-growing twiner is a

member of the bignonia family. It rises rapidly to 3–5 m and has leaves divided into numerous small leaflets which remain on the plant throughout the year except where winters are cold. It has coiling leaf tendrils which enable it to cling to a support. In summer and autumn it bears clusters of coral to orange-yellow tubular flowers 2–3 cm long. It is a pleasant screen plant, and recommended also for covering a carport or the netting around a tennis court.

CULTURE: It grows rapidly from seed and when established will survive sharp frost and some dryness. Trim and train the growing stems when necessary to keep the plant neat. In very cold regions regard it as an annual.

EUSTREPHUS LATIFOLIUS
WOMBAT BERRY

DESCRIPTION: A small evergreen twiner native to New Guinea and the warmer parts of Australia. It is not rampant in growth and therefore suitable for the small garden. The stems reach up to 3 m or a little more and are clothed with slender glossy leaves. In summer it bears clusters of small starry white or pink flowers, followed by orange berries in autumn. This is a pleasing little climber for growing in a container to ornament the patio.

CULTURE: Plant it in rich soil and partial shade and water it well during dry periods of the year. It is tender to frost.

FICUS PUMILA
CREEPING FIG,
(*Ficus repens*) TICKEY CREEPER

DESCRIPTION: Is sometimes slow in starting but once it has become established it will continue to

In a warm climate Dipladenia (*D. splendens*) grows vigorously and flowers profusely.

The bowl-shaped flowers of Bush Poppy (*Dendromecon rigida*) make a charming show in spring.

grow with cheerful abandon up a three storey building, unless checked. It is an evergreen grown for its foliage and because of its ability to cling to any surface by means of the strong rootlets on the stems. The leaves change in character as they mature. The new leaves are small and heart-shaped and make a delicate tracery against a wall. Later they become large, leathery, slightly glossy and oblong in shape. An established plant trained along a fence looks like a hedge. The cultivar 'Minima' has smaller leaves and can be more easily controlled. There is also a form with variegated leaves which makes a pretty container plant.

CULTURE: This tenacious creeper grows in shade and in sun, but in hot districts its leaves tend to turn yellow if subjected to sunshine all day. When once established it will stand considerable frost. The plant could become a nuisance, as its invasive roots tend to establish themselves in any crack in a wall and cause damage to buildings. For this reason, and because it looks best when producing new leaves, the stems should be cut back or thinned out regularly to restrict old growth and to force new growth.

FREMONTODENDRON CALIFORNICUM
(*Fremontia californica*) FREMONTIA

DESCRIPTION: Is a shrub which sends out long stems and is more effective when trained as a climber against a wall than when grown as a shrub. Allow some stems to grow to 2–3 m and cut out the others at the base, to prevent the plant from becoming bushy. It is an evergreen with lobed and unlobed leaves, dull green on the upper

The Royal Trumpet Vine (*Distictis riversii*) is a quick-growing climber with lovely flowers.

Chilean Glory Flower (*Eccremocarpus scaber*). A pretty plant for the small garden or cool patio.

Grown for its leaves, Creeping Fig (*Ficus pumila*) can be trimmed to form a piece of topiary.

Yellow Bignonia (*Doxantha unguis-cati*) looks lovely along a fence or trained up into a tree.

surface and covered with a soft brown down on the underside. In spring it bears golden-yellow, cup-shaped flowers with five petals. Each flower measures about 5 cm across.

CULTURE: It needs well-drained, gravelly soil and does not do well in regions of high humidity. Once established it stands fairly severe frost and drought.

GELSEMIUM SEMPERVIRENS

CAROLINA JASMINE

DESCRIPTION: An evergreen plant with willowy stems which may attain a height and spread of 4 m. It has ovate, shining, light green leaves up to 10 cm long which are ornamental throughout the year. In late winter and early spring it carries cascades of fragrant, golden, funnel-shaped flowers up to 3 cm long. Train it up a trellis or pillar or plant it at the top of a bank or wall and let it trail down. It is a fine plant for the small garden. All parts of this plant are said to be poisonous.

CULTURE: This is a fairly quick-growing plant which stands moderate frost but not dry conditions. If it becomes top-heavy cut it back lightly soon after flowering. Plant in good soil in sun or light shade.

GLORIOSA   FLAME LILY, GLORY LILY

DESCRIPTION: The genus includes two highly ornamental plants for gardens large and small. They grow from tubers and have a definite dormant season, and are decorative therefore only during the flowering period which is late summer. It is a good idea to plant them in the ground towards the back of a flower border or else to grow them in large pots or tubs so that they can be brought into the house or onto the patio or terrace when flowering starts. The plants send up new growth in mid-spring and attach themselves firmly to any support available, by means of tendrils at the ends of the leaves. They grow to 2–4 m. The spectacular lily-like flowers with curved petals are of a rich crimson banded with yellow. After the flowering period is over the top-growth dies back and it is therefore advisable to mark the position the plants occupy as otherwise the tubers may be damaged by careless digging in autumn and winter.

CULTURE: Plant the tuberous root stock in late winter or early spring in good, but well-drained soil, in filtered shade, setting them about 15 cm

below the surface. Over-watering the plants during their period of dormancy may cause the tubers to rot. In regions with a high winter rainfall it is advisable to plant the tubers in containers and to cover them or put them in a shed until spring. The tubers may be lifted and divided every five to eight years. They should not be disturbed until plants become overcrowded. New plants can be raised from seed but this takes three to four years to produce flowering plants. They grow in alkaline or acid soil.

G. rothschildiana   GLORY LILY

Is a native to east Africa and bears handsome flowers of crimson and gold with petals which curve gracefully out and back. It is a magnificent sight when in full flower.

G. superba   FLAME LILY

Grows wild in many parts of Rhodesia and also in South Africa, where it is often to be found flourishing in sand in coastal bush. Its flowers are not as large as those of G. rothschildiana but they are very lovely and colourful.

HARDENBERGIA COMPTONIANA

AUSTRALIAN PEA VINE, LILAC VINE

DESCRIPTION: An evergreen plant with twining stems which grow to about 3 m. The dark green leaves are an effective background throughout the year. In early spring it bears spikes of dainty violet-blue to lilac flowers. Grow it on a trellis to form a screen, train it over an arch, or let it spill down over a retaining wall. H. violacea is another species sometimes confused with this one. It is very vigorous and could become a nuisance in a small garden. Both species can be used as ground cover but will need annual trimming to keep them neat.

CULTURE: Although the Australian pea vine does best where winters are mild it will stand sharp frost. It does well in full sunshine near the coast but appears to prefer some shade in hot inland districts where dry conditions prevail. Once established it stands fairly long periods of drought. Prune, when necessary, after flowering to prevent the plant from becoming a tangled mass.

HEDERA   IVY

DESCRIPTION: Ivy has been grown in gardens for so long that a description is unnecessary. Its neat, glossy, well-shaped leaves make it a desirable evergreen plant for covering a fence or trellis, or to plant as a ground cover under trees where grass will not grow. It can be used also to cover a wall but the growth of the plant should be watched, as it may root in a tiny crack in the wall and in time cause damage. These little roots on the stems stick closely to a wall and support the plant. On the ground, branches root as they grow, and for this reason ivy is often planted as a ground cover to halt erosion, or to embellish steep banks along the roadside, or to take the place of lawn on banks where it would be difficult to mow a lawn.

CULTURE: Although the common ivy is a rampant grower it is not always easy to get it started unless one plants well-rooted cuttings. Where it is planted as a ground cover, make holes 20 cm wide and deep, about a metre apart, and fill these with rich soil to encourage fast growth. Once the plants have covered their allotted space as ground cover, trim the edges two or three times a year to prevent the roots from invading other areas. Should the plants tend to form mounds instead of a flat carpet along the ground, use a rotary lawn mower or hedge shears to cut superfluous top-growth. New leaves will soon emerge to make a neat surface. Where ivy is being grown along a trellis, wall or fence, trim top-growth all over with a pair of hedge shears once or twice a year, and head back tip-growth when it strays out of bounds. It looks most effective when trained along looped chains or wires between fence posts, or making patterns against a wall.

In hot inland gardens ivy does best in the shade. It stands severe frost and, once established, will tolerate considerable drought, but newly set out plants should be watered regularly. A dense growth of ivy is a refuge for snails and slugs so be on the alert and apply baits underneath the leaves frequently.

H. canariensis CANARY ISLAND IVY, ALGERIAN IVY

This species has very large almost heart-shaped leaves spaced further apart than those of the English ivy. The leaves are dark green, but there is a form of this species with variegated leaves marked with white, known as 'Variegata' or 'Gloire de Marengo'. These make a good ground cover on large banks and are useful also for a shady spot anywhere in the garden. The variegated cultivar is the more popular of the two for a shady place, as the variegated leaves show up better than the plain green of the species. It is often used as a container plant to ornament a shady terrace.

H. colchica PERSIAN IVY

Has large ovate glossy, leathery leaves up to 20 cm long. Because of its vigorous growth it is not recommended for the town garden of average size. 'Dentata Variegata' is a cultivar less rampant in habit and therefore more suited to the smaller garden. It has decorative foliage edged with yellow margins.

H. helix ENGLISH IVY, COMMON IVY

This is the best type to use as ground cover in the garden or to train over a form or mould, or along looped chains. It has neat, glossy, dark green, three to five-lobed leaves which remain ornamental throughout the year, and is a more suitable plant for gardens of moderate size than Algerian ivy. *H. helix* and cultivars can be trained in the fashion of topiary. Make a netting frame of the desired shape (be it a cube, mound, animal or bird) and fill it with earth and moss packed tightly. Plant several rooted cuttings and as they grow trim them to the required shape. Several hybrids, some with green leaves and some with variegated ones, have been developed for use in the garden, in hanging baskets and for indoor culture. These generally have smaller leaves than the species and they are less rampant in growth. The following are the names of a few of the many attractive cultivars:

'Buttercup'	The best of the golden forms, with leaves which become chartreuse as they age.
'Caenwoodiana'	Has small leaves with slender lobes – the central one being the longest.
'Cavendishii'	A dainty one with angular leaves margined with ivory. Pretty in a pot.
'Glacier'	Small silver-green leaves with a white margin. Lightens the shadows under a tree.
'Gold Heart'	Also referred to as 'Jubilee'. Has leaves with a pronounced splash of pale yellow in the centre.

Plant Flame Lily (*Gloriosa superba*) in a container to ornament the patio in summer.

Guinea Gold Vine (*Hibbertia scandens*) grows quickly and will brighten the garden in late spring.

'Green Ripples'	Has small leaves of unusual form – irregularly lobed, the central one being long and tapering.
'Hibernica'	Commonly known as Irish ivy. Too vigorous for the ordinary garden. Useful for large banks along roadsides.
'Marginata'	Has leaves with a broad white margin which sometimes becomes tinged with pink in winter.
'Tricolor'	A form with small jade-green leaves with a white margin which assumes a pink tinge in winter.

HIBBERTIA SCANDENS Guinea Gold Vine
(*Hibbertia volubilis*)

DESCRIPTION: An Australian plant rather shrubby in habit of growth with twining stems to 3 m or more. It has oblong, shining dark green leaves 7 cm long, which look attractive throughout the year and make a splendid foil to the bright golden-yellow flowers which festoon the plant in late spring and summer. The flowers have five rounded petals arranged like those of a single rose, ornamented in the centre with a boss of chrome-yellow stamens. This is a useful plant for making a screen in the small garden or for training up or down a bank. It looks effective also when grown in a container.

CULTURE: Grows in full sun near the coast but does best in partial shade in hot inland gardens. This is a half-hardy plant which stands moderate winters provided it has enough water. Plant in soil rich in humus and trim mature plants once a year after flowering to keep them neat.

HOYA Wax Flower

DESCRIPTION: The genus includes decorative twining plants suitable for gardens large and small, or for a patio or terrace. They are restrained in growth and have effective waxy foliage and delightful scented flowers. The flowers are produced in rounded clusters on short stems. When the flowers fade the short stems should not be removed when cutting off the dead flower, as the following season's blooms develop from them.

CULTURE: Hoya grows best in a warm, sheltered position in part shade. Established plants will stand occasional mild frosts but continued cold weather inhibits both growth and flowering. They appear to do better when planted in a container under shelter than out-of-doors, and potbound plants often flower better than those in the garden. Plant them in well-drained soil rich in humus and water well in summer. Allow plants to go dormant in winter by reducing the water given.

H. bella

Is native to India and Malaya and requires warm conditions. It sends up slender stems with small

74

leaves and bears tight clusters of sweetly-scented, waxy white flowers with a starry face, in summer. It is at its best in a pot or a hanging basket.

H. carnosa

This is a more vigorous species from Australia, and a most desirable plant. Its stems grow to 2–3 m and carry thick, waxy oval leaves 5–8 cm long. The lovely rounded clusters of scented flowers also look as though they have been fashioned from wax. They are creamy white to pink, with a pink star-shaped ornament in the centre of each flower. The flowering time is summer. Whether grown indoors or out, the stems should be trained to a support. There is a cultivar with leaves flushed with creamy-white but it is not easy to propagate or grow.

HYDRANGEA   CLIMBING HYDRANGEAS

DESCRIPTION: The shrubby hydrangeas are well-known and most useful plants for the garden and for arrangements, but the climbing types are little known and seldom grown, yet, they too are deserving of space in gardens where conditions are congenial to their growth. Three species, two of which are deciduous, are described below. They will grow to 4 m or more, but can be trimmed to reduce their spread.

CULTURE: These plants enjoy cold and are not at their best in hot humid gardens. Generally they require much the same conditions as the common garden hydrangea – namely – good soil which is slightly acid in nature, an abundance of compost about their roots, shade or part shade and water throughout the year. They may develop slowly during the first two or three years, but once the roots are firmly established and provided they are watered well, they will grow rapidly.

H. anomala

Is a climber for the large garden and looks its best when climbing up into tall trees. The leaves are coarsely toothed, ovate in form and dark green in colour. The flowers which appear in late spring do not make a spectacular show but are of some merit.

H. integerrima

This is a self-clinging evergreen species with obovate leathery leaves. In summer it bears large

Convolvulus (Ipomoea) can be relied on to produce a mass of lovely flowers under adverse conditions.

clusters of creamy-white flowers. It is grown for its foliage effect rather than for the flowers, although on mature plants these can make a fine show.

H. petiolaris
Of the climbing hydrangeas this species bears the most handsome flowers. They are ivory and appear in summer in flat panicles measuring about 20 cm across, and are rather like the flowers of the 'lace-cap' hydrangea. It is deciduous and clings firmly by means of aerial rootlets to any support – be it a tree or a wall.

IPOMOEA
MORNING GLORY, CONVOLVULUS AND OTHERS

DESCRIPTION: This is a large genus – of more than 400 twining or creeping evergreen and deciduous plants, most of which are native to the warmer countries of the world. Many of them are invaluable in the garden for making a quick temporary screen, and some of them are of permanent ornamental value – twining up a pillar, against a wall, as a ground cover, or draped over an unsightly shed. A few of them are good plants for hanging baskets or pots. The leaves of most species make an attractive cover and the flowers are invariably very pretty. They may be funnel- or bell-shaped, or tubular.

CULTURE: The annuals grow quickly from seed sown in spring and will flower in three to four months of sowing. Soak the seed for several hours to speed up germination. Perennial types are usually grown from cuttings made in spring. These may take a year to produce flowering plants. They grow in full sun or part shade. Perennial species are tender to sharp frost and in cold gardens should be protected. Often, although the top growth may be frozen to the ground, the roots will remain alive, particularly if a thick mulch has been put around them. Where frosts do not kill off the top-growth it is advisable to cut the plants back in autumn to keep them within bounds.

I. acuminata
BLUE CONVOLVULUS

Rapidly twines its way across 6 m and may spread further if not checked. It has heart-shaped or three-lobed leaves and bluish-purple flowers 6 cm long. It dies down during the cool months but reappears in spring. Can become a pest because of its rampant growth.

I. biloba
(*I. pes-caprae*)

Is a trailing perennial confined to tropical beaches. It is of no value in the garden but included here as it is a useful plant to stop the drift of sand along the coast. The lobed ovate or obovate leaves are thick and rather fleshy, 5–10 cm in length and often broader than long. The small flowers are pink to purple. The plant may grow to 5 m on a trellis or across the ground.

I. horsfalliae
CARDINAL CREEPER

A showy evergreen twiner from the West Indies which, if left to its own devices, will climb to 6–9 m or more. The leaves are thick and divided into several lobes or else into leaflets. The flowers appear in profusion in summer. Each one is made up of a broad tube opening to a starry face about 5 cm across. The colour is a rich lustrous rose to coral-red.

I. learii
BLUE DAWN FLOWER

The common name is very apt, for each morning new flowers of sky-blue open and brighten the garden. In the late afternoon they fade away, but each summer morning another profusion of blue will greet the day. It is quick and vigorous, particularly under subtropical conditions, where, if not restrained, it will soon cover 12 m or more.

I. purpurea
MORNING GLORY

This twiner is regarded as a pest by some and a blessing by others. Once it gets into the garden it is difficult to eradicate because, although the top growth dies down in winter, it emerges again in spring and spreads itself rapidly across neighbouring plants. The large purple flowers are borne in great profusion all summer long. It is a useful plant for making a verdant show in gardens which are dry in summer, or for covering unsightly outbuildings, ugly fences or railway or road embankments, but its spread should be controlled.

I. quamoclit
CYPRESS VINE
(*Quamoclit pinnata*)

A quick-growing annual which reaches a height of 2 m in 3–4 months. The leaves are light green and quite different from those of the convolvulus usually seen in gardens. They are finely divided and form a pretty background to the flowers which appear in summer. The flower consists of a long tube opening to a salver-shaped face of five segments. Their colour is red shaded with yellow in the throat. This is a good creeper for temporary cover on a fence. Sow seed or set out plants in spring after frosts are over.

I. tricolor   Morning Glory
(*I. rubro-caerulea*)

Probably the most popular of the morning glories. It is a perennial but best treated as an annual. It grows readily from seed sown in spring and, where it has sufficient warmth and moisture, it will cover a fence or wall to 6 m in four or five months. The heart-shaped leaves are decorative and the flowers are very lovely. They are funnel-shaped at the base and open to a trumpet-like face of translucent blue with delicate wedge-shaped bands of a paler colour. It is native to Mexico, where it is reported that the seeds are chewed for their hallucinogenic properties. 'Flying Saucers', with flowers striped blue and white, and 'Heavenly Blue' are two lovely cultivars derived from this.

I. tuberosa   Wood Rose

This species is curious rather than beautiful. It is a tuberous-rooted climber which is vigorous and will climb rapidly in sun or shade. The leaves are palmately lobed and the flowers are funnel-shaped and of a creamy-yellow hue. After the flowers fade the sepals enlarge and spread out, and these together with the fruit resemble a wooden flower, which accounts for the common name. They are useful for dried arrangements.

JASMINUM   Jasmine, Jessamine

Description: The genus includes a wide diversity of plants – shrubs, climbers and twiners – some evergreen and some deciduous; and it provides us with the most sweetly-scented of all plants. Not all of them, however, have a delightful fragrance. Some lack scent altogether. There are species which like shade and others which grow in full sunshine. They can be used as ground covers, for training against the walls of a building, along a fence to form a hedge or screen, on a trellis or arbour, over an old tree stump, or to cover a bank. The flowers are usually tubular, opening to a starry face and are generally white or yellow in colour.

Culture: Some jasmines tolerate severe cold and some thrive only in warm areas. Details of climatic conditions which suit them are given under the different species here described. Plant in good soil and water the young plants to establish a robust root system. It is advisable to start thinning out or trimming jasmines quite early in life to prevent them from forming a tangle of growth. The best time to do this is immediately after they have flowered, but it can be done at any other time of the year without harm to the plants. It may, however, delay flowering.

J. angulare   East London Jasmine

Is a charming twining shrub native to warm coastal regions of South Africa. It is evergreen with pretty, glossy trifoliate leaves. In spring and early summer it bears clusters of dainty waxy-white flowers with a delightful scent. It will stand only moderate frost. Where winters are cold plant it in a large container which can be moved to a sheltered spot during winter. Grown in a container it remains small and is an attractive plant to embellish the patio.

J. azoricum   Azores Jasmine

A choice twining species from the island of Madeira. It has shining trifoliate leaves and clusters of sweetly-scented flowers in spring. They are flushed with purple in the bud but open to pure white. In a region where frosts are mild it will flourish in the garden. Where frosts are severe plant it in a pot or in a protected corner against a wall which reflects warmth during winter. Water during winter to encourage good flowering.

J. beesianum

A shrubby species with willowy stems to 3 m. The leaves are slender and mid-green in colour. Small fragrant crimson to carmine flowers appear in spring. They are not showy but this is a useful plant for a cold garden as it enjoys frosty winters.

J. dispersum

A fine species from north India. It has leaves divided into three leaflets and clusters of fragrant white flowers flushed with pink. The main flowering time is late spring and early summer. Stands moderate frost.

J. floridum

This is a scandent or sprawling evergreen plant. It grows to 1,5 m and carries leaves divided into three small leaflets. In spring it bears clusters of yellow flowers which have no scent at all. It is not as pretty as many other jasmines but it is hardy to severe frost.

The sweetly-scented flowers of African Jasmine (*Jasminum multipartitum*) appear in spring.

J. mesnyi PRIMROSE JASMINE
(*J. primulinum*)

This evergreen scandent shrub produces an abundance of slender stems which arch out gracefully. It looks effective when planted as a hedge but the stems can be trained up a trellis, over a bank, or against a wall. The leaves are divided into three leaflets of a pleasant shade of apple-green, and in winter the plant becomes festooned with small bright golden-yellow, semi-double flowers. It tolerates severe frost and, once established, endures long periods without water, too. It is, therefore, a useful plant for regions where a harsh climate makes gardening difficult. It will grow in full sun or part shade. If grown as a climber, cut out some of the stems which come up from ground level and tie the others to a support. It needs trimming once a year to keep it neat.

J. multipartitum AFRICAN JASMINE
A delightful and lovable plant which can be trained up a wall, along a fence, over an arch or pergola, or trimmed to shrub size. It has lustrous, dark green leaves which are decorative throughout the year, and from spring to summer it bears a magnanimous profusion of waxy-white, sweetly-scented flowers which show up beautifully against the dark green of the leaves. The unopened bud, neatly furled like an umbrella, is tinged with claret. The flower consists of a long slender tube opening to a starry face 4 cm across. Sprigs of this jasmine are delightful in arrangements as the buds open after they are picked and their scent pervades the house. It stands occasional drops in temperature to freezing but does best in regions which have mild winters. Once established it will endure long periods with little water.

J. nudiflorum WINTER JASMINE
Winter jasmine, like primrose jasmine, described above, is a useful plant to introduce colour in very cold gardens at a season when little is in flower. It is not as decorative as primrose jasmine as it loses its leaves in autumn and it is more of a rambling shrub than a true climber. In winter it has yellow flowers with no fragrance. When the flowers begin to fade the new green leaves appear. The plant grows to a height of 4 m and can be trained against a wall or pegged down to cascade over a bank. It does best in cool gardens and in partial shade. Cut back the flowering stems immediately after flowering is over to keep the

Laburnum vossii is a small tree which looks splendid when trained as a climber.

plant tidy and to encourage new flowering stems to develop.

J. officinale   COMMON JASMINE, POET'S JASMINE
A climbing, twining plant which grows to 9 m. It may lose all its leaves in cold districts but is evergreen where winters are mild. The flowers which appear in clusters in summer are pinkish in the bud and white when open, with the sweetest of scents. This plant stands cold and a good deal of dryness when established. Plant it where it can climb up into a tree, or be trained over a trellis or pergola. Watch it, as it is all too eager to embrace the entire garden, and prune it hard as soon as it shows signs of getting out of hand. A cultivar 'Aureo Variegatum' has leaves suffused with creamy-yellow. It is not as vigorous in growth as the species.

J. polyanthum   CHINESE JASMINE
Is the most popular and ornamental of the jasmines. It is a fast-growing, evergreen climbing or twining plant to a height of 6 m or more. The glossy leaves are divided into five to seven oval, pointed leaflets which remain attractive throughout the year. In late winter and early spring the plant dons its lovely mantle of fragrant flowers which are pink in the bud and ivory tinged with pink when open. Although the flowers are small they are carried in large clusters and in such abundance that it is a spectacular sight when in full flower. It is native to China and stands quite considerable frost but does not do well unless watered regularly. Where winters are severe try growing it in a protected position on the north wall of the house. Under optimum conditions it becomes rampant in growth and it should therefore be trimmed back annually to keep it from tangling. Do this immediately after flowering is over, by cutting out some shoots at the base and shortening others. This is a fine plant to train up a trellis, around a post, along a fence, over a pergola, against a wall, or to have hanging like a curtain over a bank or balcony.

Chinese Jasmine (*Jasminum polyanthum*). A quick-growing twiner with charming, sweetly-scented flowers.

Honeysuckle (Lonicera) enjoys cold conditions and produces an abundance of fragrant flowers.

J. sambac   ARABIAN JASMINE
The common name is a misnomer as this evergreen plant is native to India. It is a shrub rather than a climber but if some of the stems are thinned out and others trained against a wall it makes an effective show. It is an evergreen, popular in many of the warm countries. In Hawaii it is used in leis, in China, for making jasmine-scented tea, and in other countries for perfume. The white, starry flowers are small but have a strong and delicious scent. They appear mostly in spring but it has some flowers during other seasons of the year too. The leaves are slightly glossy, ovate in form and up to 5 cm long. It tolerates mild frost.

J. x stephanense   CHINESE JASMINE
A hybrid of vigorous growth to 8 m. It is evergreen in a mild climate but will lose most of its leaves in regions where winters are cold. The leaves may be simple or divided into five leaflets. Tiny pale pink flowers with a haunting scent appear in late spring and early summer.

KENNEDIA   CORAL VINE, TWINING PEA
DESCRIPTION: The genus includes a number of twining plants native to different parts of Australia, three of which are worth growing in the garden. They are good plants for quick cover. The leaves are divided into three to five leaflets and the pea-like flowers are purple to burgundy or coral-red in colour. They are useful as ground cover over a dry bank or as twining plants along a fence or over a trellis.
CULTURE: When established they will stand moderate frost and long periods with little water. If frost cuts them back they usually grow out again, particularly if a thick mulch of straw has been put over the ground to protect the roots. They grow readily from seed which should be soaked for a few hours to speed up germination. Plant in full sun in well-drained soil.

K. coccinea   CORAL VINE
Has trailing stems of mid-green leaflets. In early spring it wears a colourful cloak of bright coral-red flowers. The upper segment is marked with a yellow spot edged with deep purple. It grows to 3–4 m and is an effective cover for a road or railway embankment or for a dry bank in the garden. It looks attractive also when trained up around a post to form a column of red when in flower.

K. nigricans
This is not a particularly attractive plant but its trailing stems make a quick screen or ground cover. The leaves may be simple or trifoliate. The flowers of dark violet appear in the greatest profusion in late winter and early spring. The standard (upper segment) is blotched with pale yellow. This is a useful plant for hot dry gardens which have moderate frost, but watch it, and be ready with secateurs to cut it back hard, after its flowering period is over, or it may take over a good deal of the garden.

K. rubicunda
A vigorous evergreen twiner with leaves divided into three broadly ovate leaflets 5–6 cm long. The flowers which appear in spring are crimson. This species does well in seaside gardens, and in dry gardens inland.

LABLAB PURPUREUS   SUDANESE BEAN,
(*Dolichos lablab*)   HYACINTH BEAN
DESCRIPTION: Is a slender, twining plant worth growing where quick, temporary cover is needed. It is an annual which grows to a height of 2–3 m between spring and summer. The leaves of mid-green are heart-shaped or broadly ovate and make a pleasing background to the purple, pea-shaped flowers which appear in late summer and autumn. When the flowers fade the plant is covered with large pods rather like those of a bean. These are relished by some African tribes.
CULTURE: It is native to the tropics and although it can be grown in cold regions it is inadvisable to set out plants or to sow seed until all danger of frost is over in spring. It thrives in a sunny position.

LABURNUM VOSSII   LABURNUM
DESCRIPTION: This is a small deciduous tree which is a glory to behold when it flowers well. It can be trained as a climber and as such it makes an impressive show grown along a pergola in a large garden or park. In the small garden a single specimen could be trained to fan out against a wall. It has trifoliate greyish-green leaves which are of some ornamental value for most of the year. In late winter or early spring, pea-shaped flowers carried in long cascading skeins, like those of a wisteria, appear in magnificent profusion, creating a shining mantle of gold.
CULTURE: Laburnum is not for the hot dry

garden. It enjoys cold frosty winters and wants good soil and an abundance of moisture throughout the year. In inland gardens, where the sun is excessively bright, plant it in partial or open shade – against the south wall of the house.

LAPAGERIA ROSEA CHILEAN BELLFLOWER

DESCRIPTION: This is the national flower of Chile and well deserves this honour, for it is a striking plant when in flower. It is an evergreen climber with slender twining stems to 2–3 m. The glossy leaves are heart-shaped at the base tapering sharply to a point, leathery in texture and up to 2 cm in length. In summer it bears hanging, bell-shaped flowers made up of six separate segments. They are waxy in texture, about 6–10 cm long and of a warm, glowing rose-red colour. They last well when cut for arrangements. Tie the stems to a trellis as they grow. A cultivar 'Albiflora' has pure white flowers.

CULTURE: Chilean bellflower is not easy to grow. It is particular both as to soil and situation. It needs shade, rich acid soil and an abundance of water. This is not a plant for tropical areas nor for regions which have long periods of hot dry weather. It does well where winters are cool, provided the atmosphere is not dry. Plant it in shade.

LATHYRUS SWEET PEA

DESCRIPTION: The genus includes a large number of annual and perennial plants, many of which are climbers or twiners which support themselves by means of tendrils. The leaves are pinnate, that is, divided into several leaflets. The flowers, like all pea flowers, are composed of a large upright rounded petal (standard or banner), two narrow side petals (wings) and two lower petals, sometimes united, (the keel). They are decorative in gardens large and small and for flower arrangements too. Provide supports for the plants. The perennial type is not as attractive as the annual ones.

CULTURE: These are deep-rooting plants and it is therefore advisable to prepare a hole or trench 30 cm deep, and to incorporate plenty of compost or manure with the soil in the trench. Both the popular annual and perennial forms grow readily from seed. Soak seed for a few hours before sowing to speed up germination. The plants will come into flower four to six months afterwards.

L. grandiflorus

An annual from southern Europe with leaves divided into a pair of oval leaflets of mid-green. In late spring and early summer it is a lovely sight – covered with large flowers of rose to cyclamen hue. It grows to about 2 m in height and is therefore suitable for the small garden.

L. latifolius EVERLASTING PEA

A perennial twiner which reaches a height of 2–3 m. Its leaves are divided into two slender leaflets. The flowers are fairly large and rosy-purple, pink or white in colour. A useful plant for covering a bank.

L. odoratus SWEET PEA

Is the annual type loved by gardeners throughout the world. Few plants produce flowers with greater appeal, lovely in the garden and in arrangements. Their ethereal beauty is matched by their delicate sweet scent. Sweet peas have the additional merit of not needing much space and a few plants can easily be raised in the smallest of gardens. There are several strains and hundreds of cultivars of great beauty. Generally they are at their best when sown in late summer for flowers in late winter and early spring, but where severe frosts occur and summers are not excessively warm, spring-sowing is recommended.

L. splendens PRIDE OF CALIFORNIA

Is shrubby in form with twining stems. It seldom grows to more than a metre, and is useful for a rock garden or as a ground cover. Its leaves are divided into two or three pairs of leaflets which give it a graceful appearance. Clusters of rose to cyclamen flowers highlight the plant in summer.

LONICERA HONEYSUCKLE

DESCRIPTION: Honeysuckles have been popular for hundreds of years. They figure in the old Greek and Roman ornamentation on buildings. They were used in magic, and they were often referred to in prose and poetry. In Shakespeare's day the common honeysuckle was known as woodbine – an emblem of faithfulness. It was much used also in medicine – the seed for stomach trouble, and a preparation from the flowers as a lotion for the skin. The honeysuckles include deciduous and evergreen climbers and shrubs of scrambling growth – many of which have fragrant flowers. Generally the ones with scent have the least colourful flowers. These are useful plants for camouflaging unsightly corners, or planting on banks, or for making a screen or hedge. The flowers are tubular, often with recurved lips.

CULTURE: Most of them are hardy, putting up with freezing weather in winter. They will also endure short periods with little water, but under dry conditions their growth will be restricted. Honeysuckles do well in sun or semi-shade, and some species can be grown as a ground cover under tall trees. When grown as a ground cover they should be sheared off every year or two to keep the top-growth neat. They require soil rich in humus.

L. x americana

A vigorous twining deciduous plant which reaches 5 m. The oval or obovate leaves are 3–10 cm long. Several of the upper pairs are united. The scented flowers are carried in whorls. They are ivory at first, turning yellow suffused with rosy-purple as they age, and are most profuse in late spring and early summer.

L. x brownii   SCARLET HONEYSUCKLE

A charming climber for the small garden. It is not as exuberant in growth as the other species, reaching a height of 2–3 m with sparse side branches. Its leaves are ovate or obovate 2–6 cm long, the upper pairs being united. The gay ruby-red flowers, which appear in profusion in spring, are decorative but not scented. This plant is evergreen where winters are mild but may lose most of its leaves where winters are cold.

L. caprifolium   COMMON HONEYSUCKLE

A twining evergreen or deciduous plant which can be kept trimmed to bush form. It has yellowish-white, two-lipped flowers carried in bunches or whorls. They are very sweetly-scented, but not particularly showy. The upper leaves are united to form a saucer.

L. x heckrottii   CORAL HONEYSUCKLE

This quick-growing plant is deciduous in cold areas and evergreen in warm climates. It grows to 3 m or more but can be kept trimmed back to smaller size. The flowers appear in clusters in spring to summer. They are 4–5 cm in length, coral pink on the outside and yellow inside. Some lovely named hybrids have been developed from this one. 'Gold Flame' has flowers coloured orange outside and golden-yellow on the inside. Trained along a fence it makes a good screen.

Although Luculia is shrubby in habit it can be trimmed and trained as a climber.

Mandevilla has slender stems and masses of glorious, sweetly-scented flowers in summer.

L. hildebrandiana
GIANT BURMESE HONEYSUCKLE

A rampant evergreen reaching a height of 6 m or more, with glossy, dark green ovate leaves 7–15 cm long, and clusters of large tubular flowers which open white or creamy-yellow and change to rich yellow, sometimes flushed with orange. Its fragrant blooms appear in late spring and early summer. This plant is tender to severe frost but does well in warm regions. It is a good plant to cover a fence around a large property or to train into a tall tree. It has the largest leaves and flowers of all the honeysuckles and is too vigorous for the small garden.

L. japonica
JAPANESE HONEYSUCKLE

An evergreen twining plant which is partly deciduous when subjected to severe cold. It is too robust in growth for the small garden. The sweetly-fragrant flowers carried in pairs are white, becoming tinged with purple and yellow as they age. Hybrids developed from this one are now more popular than the species. *L. japonica* 'Aureo-reticulata' (Variegated Honeysuckle) has leaves which are attractively veined with yellow. *L. japonica* 'Halliana' (Hall's Honeysuckle) is a particularly vigorous cultivar – useful as a ground cover in large gardens or on embankments. Once established it endures drought and cold. Needs to be kept in check to limit its spread and top-growth.

L. periclymenum
WOODBINE

A hardy deciduous twining plant to 6 m. It has broad oval or obovate leaves, dark green on the upper surface and paler beneath. The flowers, which appear in clusters in late spring, are claret on the outside and ivory to pale yellow inside and very fragrant. 'Belgica' (spring-flowering) and 'Serotina' (summer-flowering) are two good cultivars, more attractive than the species.

L. sempervirens
RED HONEYSUCKLE

This is an evergreen which can be trained as a shrub or given support to help it climb. The flowers lack the sweet scent characteristic of honeysuckles but they are colourful. Arranged in charming clusters the bright coral-red tubular flowers make a gay display. It is hardy to severe frost.

L. x tellmanniana

Does well in shade or semi-shade and can be grown as a climber to 6 m or trained to shrub-shape. It is deciduous or evergreen depending on climate, with showy clusters of tubular flowers 5 cm long. They are a warm coppery red in the bud and golden-yellow when open. The flowering time is late spring and early summer. It stands cold but needs shade and moisture.

L. tragophylla
CHINESE HONEYSUCKLE

Although the flowers are not fragrant this species is highly ornamental and worth growing in the large garden. It is a hardy deciduous climber which does best in moist soil and semi-shade. In spring to early summer it bears large clusters of golden-yellow flowers. Let it grow up into a tree or plant it against the south wall of the house. It will reach 6 m in height.

Barclay Maurandia will flower within six months from seed sown in spring.

Maurandia erubescens. A quick-growing climber for gardens small and large.

LUCULIA GRATISSIMA · LUCULIA

DESCRIPTION: A shrubby plant which, with some thinning and training, can be grown as a wall plant or along a fence. Tie some of the longer shoots up over an arch or fix them against a wall, and trim out others at the base to prevent the plant from taking up too much space laterally. This is an evergreen which makes a gorgeous show in autumn. It has handsome ovate mid-green leaves and circular heads of lovely fragrant shell-pink flowers. The individual flower consists of a slender tube which terminates in a flat face of five rounded segments.

L. grandifolia is a species of more vigorous growth with leaves up to 30 cm long and pure white fragrant flowers.

CULTURE: Luculia is not an easy plant to grow, but it is very beautiful. This together with its scent and the fact that it flowers in autumn, makes it worth taking trouble to give it the conditions it requires. Plant it in rich soil where it is shaded from the afternoon sun and water it well, particularly during dry periods of the year. It is hardy to moderate frost but not dry conditions.

MANDEVILLA LAXA · CHILEAN JASMINE
(*M. suaveolens*)

DESCRIPTION: This deciduous plant is one of the most decorative of the climbers with white flowers. Once established it grows quickly to 6 m. It has broad leaves pointed at the apex and heart-shaped at the base. In late spring and summer lovely clusters of waxy-white flowers appear – festooning the plant luxuriantly, and perfuming the air with their rich gardenia-like scent. Each flower consists of a tube ending in five segments. Mandevilla will attach itself to the branches of a tree by means of its twining stems. It makes a pretty sight, too, growing over a trellis or patio. It is unfortunately not attractive in winter and should be planted with an evergreen climber which will hide its bare untidy stems.

CULTURE: Mandevilla may be cut down by frost, but, if the root area is covered with a thick mulch of straw, the root itself may not be damaged, and the plant usually grows up again in spring. It is hardy to 5° of frost. In hot inland gardens plant it where it has some shade from overhanging trees or the house, and water during dry periods of the year. It grows readily from seed. Trim and train established plants in winter to prevent them from becoming a tangle.

MANETTIA BICOLOR · MANETTIA

DESCRIPTION: A quick-growing evergreen twining plant to about 2 m, suitable for a small wall or trellis or to grow in a pot on a balcony. It is native to Brazil, and has pretty leaves – broad at the base and pointed at the apex, with clear veins. From the axils of the leaves slender stems emerge carrying charming little flowers 2–3 cm long. They are tubular in form, scarlet at the base and sulphur-yellow at the tips. The main flowering season is spring but it has some flowers throughout the year.

CULTURE: It grows in any kind of soil but needs warmth and humidity for its best development. In hot gardens inland plant it in shade.

MAURANDYA BARCLAIANA
(*Asarina barclaiana*) · BARCLAY MAURANDIA, MAURANDIA

DESCRIPTION: A dainty evergreen Mexican climber which grows to 3 m. The plant has a twining stem and leaves which are heart- or arrow-shaped at the base. It attaches itself to a support by twining the leaf stems about the stake or other plants. The purple flowers, somewhat like those of a bignonia, appear in summer and autumn. Other species worth trying are *M. antirrihiniflora*, *M. erubescens* and *M. lophospermum* (sometimes called the climbing foxglove).

CULTURE: Maurandia is a useful plant for providing quick cover as it will grow to 2 m in a few months, from seed sown when the weather is warm in spring. Once established it will stand moderate frost, but the top-growth may die down in winter. It likes an abundance of sunshine and is tolerant of fairly long dry periods.

METROSIDEROS CARMINEA · RATA VINE

DESCRIPTION: A pretty little New Zealand plant which attaches itself to a wall or fence by means of aerial roots – rather like ivy. It can also be trained over an old tree stump or over boulders. The leaves are small and oval in form. In summer and autumn it becomes wreathed in clusters of little cornelian-red flowers with prominent curved stamens. In its native habitat it will climb to the tops of tall trees but may not reach more than 2–3 m in the garden.

CULTURE: Once established it stands long periods of cold but it needs regular watering to encourage growth. In a hot dry garden plant it in partial shade.

84

MONSTERA DELICIOSA

DELICIOUS MONSTER

DESCRIPTION: An unusual Mexican plant often grown in a pot indoors or on a patio or terrace. It is an evergreen with large and handsome leaves. The juvenile leaves are glossy and pale green whilst the older leaves are dark with large perforations which add to their handsome appearance. The flower is composed of a huge ivory spathe, like a conch shell in shape, which surrounds the flower parts. The cylindrical fruits (16–20 cm long) have the smell and flavour of a fruit salad. These are edible but unfortunately they have invisible prickly cells which tend to make eating unpleasant, until the fleshy sections fall away. The tip of the cylinder ripens about a week before the base which also detracts from the possibility of using the fruit as a delicacy. Plants in pots seldom flower, but those in the garden bloom at various times of the year. The leaves are useful for large arrangements. Grow it in a container indoors or in a shady place outside, or plant it against the bole of a tree which will support the stem and give it shade. Under optimum conditions it will climb to 6 m. Long cord-like roots on the stems help to anchor the plant and they give rise to new plants too.

CULTURE: Monstera likes soil rich in humus and shade. It tolerates moderate frost. Where severe frosts are likely to occur grow it as an indoor plant.

MUCUNA BENNETTII

FLAME OF THE FOREST CREEPER, MUCUNA

DESCRIPTION: This is one of the most spectacular of all climbing plants. It occurs naturally in the rain forests of Malaysia, where it may be seen growing into tall trees, creating glowing masses of colour in the topmost branches. The leaves, almost as broad as they are long, make rich curtains of green. The plant belongs to the same family as the pea and has flowers somewhat similar in form. They are brilliantly coloured and carried in opulent trusses which hang down creating a magnificent mantle of coral-red in late autumn and early winter. There are two other decorative species from the tropics: – *M. albertisii* and *M. novoguiniensis*, both of which are native to New Guinea.

CULTURE: These rare and lovely plants need warm humid conditions, good soil and shelter from drying winds. They should therefore be tried only in tropical and subtropical gardens. They can be grown from seed or cuttings.

MUEHLENBECKIA COMPLEXA

WIRE VINE

DESCRIPTION: An evergreen climbing or creeping plant native to New Zealand, with slender wiry stems of romping habit, carrying an abundance of tiny leaves. With support it will climb to 6 m, and, without support, it forms a carpet of leaves along the ground. When trained on netting and clipped occasionally it makes a pleasing screen of foliage. It is a useful plant for covering bare tree stumps and rocky banks, and for use as a ground cover over a large area. It has white flowers which are not showy but which have a scent.

CULTURE: This is a strong-rooting little plant which, once established, will stand both cold and dryness. It does well in coastal gardens, surviving salt-laden wind.

OXERA PULCHELLA   OXERA

DESCRIPTION: An evergreen climber from New Caledonia which puts on a fine show where conditions are congenial. It may grow to 8 m in its natural home, but seldom reaches more than 2–3 m in the garden. The leaves are lance-shaped or oblong and up to 10 cm in length, sometimes with scalloped edges. The clusters of ivory-white, lightly-scented flowers appear in spring, and occasionally in autumn, too. The individual flowers are funnel-shaped with four lobes and two protruding stamens.

CULTURE: A plant suitable for warm coastal gardens where there is humidity in the air. In the hot interior plant it in partial shade, in good soil, and water abundantly.

PANDOREA   BOWER VINE,
WONGA-WONGA VINE

DESCRIPTION: The two plants of this genus which are popular as garden subjects are both evergreen climbers from Australia with attractive foliage and pretty trumpet-shaped flowers. The leaves are divided into glossy leaflets which are decorative throughout the year. The plants climb by twining themselves around a support. They are admirable ones to make a screen for privacy, or for protection against wind, and they look effective also clambering over a bank, around a pillar or on a trellis.

When allowed to spread or climb, Monstera produces its unusual shell-shaped flowers.

Mucuna (*M. bennettii*) is a gorgeous climber for a humid tropical garden.

CULTURE: Both species described will stand fairly sharp frost but not prolonged periods of freezing weather. If planted in rich soil and watered abundantly they will prove quick-growers. They do well in sun or partial shade, at the coast or inland.

P. jasminoides BOWER VINE
(*Bignonia jasminoides*)
A fast-growing evergreen climber to 4 m with graceful stems of attractive shining dark green leaves, composed of five to nine oval pointed leaflets, 2–8 cm long. The flowers, which festoon the plant in summer, are funnel-shaped, ending in an open face of five rounded segments. They are white flushed with cornelian-red in the throat. It has tendrils which help to attach the plant to any support. Cultivars with flowers of other colours have recently been introduced. The one with shell-pink flowers is particularly enchanting. This plant does best in warm districts, but it will flourish in areas of moderate frost too. If frost cuts it back it generally grows up quickly again in spring, and will produce a mass of flowers before summer is over.

P. pandorana WONGA-WONGA VINE
(*Bignonia australis*)
This species stands less cold than *P. jasminoides*, and it is not as decorative. It is a vigorous plant which reaches a height of 6 m with stems densely clothed with glossy foliage which is pretty throughout the year. The flowers are less than 3 cm in length and creamy-white spotted with maroon inside. The wonga-wonga vine makes a dense hedge if trained along a boundary fence and clipped occasionally to keep it neat.

PARTHENOCISSUS VIRGINIA CREEPER,
(*Ampelopsis*) BOSTON IVY
DESCRIPTION: The genus includes climbers of tremendous virility, which will climb a church steeple or a tree 30 m high. They have been grown for generations because of their hardiness and the beauty of their foliage. The leaves are pretty in form and colour, and in autumn they assume warm shades of burnished copper and crimson before dropping. They have the additional attribute of being self-supporting, clinging to any support handy by means of tendrils, or to a wall

Virginia Creeper (*Parthenocissus tricuspidata*) makes a splendid show in autumn.

Parthenocissus quinquefolia is another form of Virginia Creeper with lovely autumnal colour.

with sucker-like discs. Unfortunately these will not always adhere to walls which have been painted. Their one disadvantage is that they tend to become too invasive unless kept in check. CULTURE: The species described tolerate a wide range of growing conditions. They endure intense cold and will also grow fairly well in hot dry places. They thrive in partial shade and in full sunlight, and can be grown up a wall or fence or allowed to spread across the ground. They are not suited to tropical or sub-tropical conditions.

P. henryana   CHINESE VIRGINIA CREEPER
A self-clinging species with delightful leaves made up of three to five narrow oval or obovate leaflets which are deep green, with white and pink along the midrib and main veins. They turn fiery colours before dropping in autumn. Grow it in shade against a wall. It is slow-growing, but this is an advantage in a small garden.

P. himalayana HIMALAYAN VIRGINIA CREEPER
This species is similar to the Virginia creeper but has larger leaflets arranged in threes. The tendrils

have adhesive pads which enable it to cling to a wall without support. It bears purplish-blue fruits and has good autumnal colour, particularly in regions where the autumn is frosty.

P. inserta
A vigorous climber with strong tendrils. The leaves, divided into five shiny, sharply-toothed, obovate leaflets, assume rich colours in autumn. It differs from Virginia creeper in that its tendrils do not have adhesive pads at the tips. Looks effective on a wall, in a tree, or along a pergola. It grows to 6 m or more.

P. quinquefolia   VIRGINIA CREEPER
This species sometimes takes a year to settle down, but, once the roots are established it grows with cheerful abandon sending its stems of attractive leaves far and wide, clinging to any handy support or a wall by means of its adhesive pads. The leaves, divided into three or five ovate or obovate leaflets with toothed margins, turn lovely autumn colours. Plant it against a wall, at the base of a tree, or as a ground cover on a slope. It should be trimmed back once a year to keep it within

87

bounds. A cultivar known as 'Engelmannii' has smaller leaves and is less invasive.

P. tricuspidata — BOSTON IVY, VIRGINIA CREEPER

This semi-evergreen climber stands extremely low temperatures, but loses most of its leaves in cold gardens. It has glossy leaves up to 20 cm wide, which are variable in form – often ovate on young plants and three-lobed on older plants. In areas which have hot dry weather this species should be tried on the south side of a building or beneath trees where it is shaded. In cold areas the leaves become a glorious, scintillating scarlet in autumn. It is one of the most popular of deciduous climbers because of its rich autumnal colour and self-clinging nature. The cultivar known as 'Veitchii' has smaller leaves than the species.

PASSIFLORA — PASSION FLOWER, GRANADILLA

DESCRIPTION: The genus includes about 500 species, many of which are climbers of vigorous growth. Some are evergreen whilst others are semi-evergreen or deciduous. Because of their exuberant growth they need to be trimmed back regularly to prevent them from becoming a tangled mass. The plants embrace any support at hand, including neighbouring plants, by means of their strong tendrils.

The flower consists of a short tube which opens to a saucer-shaped flower of 5 sepals and 5 petals – all of which look much the same and are referred to as tepals. Inside is the corona which is made up of rings of thread-like filaments, often prettily coloured. The five stamens are arranged on a central column, above which is the ovary and three stigmas. The fruits vary in shape and size and contain numerous seeds embedded in a thick pulp. In regions with short cool summers the plants are unlikely to form fruits.

The name of 'Passion Flower' originated many years ago amongst the Spanish priests of South America, who saw, in the parts of the flower, symbols of Christ's passion and crucifixion. The three stigmas represent the three nails; the five stamens the five wounds; the ten tepals (5 sepals and 5 petals) represent the ten faithful apostles – Judas and Peter being absent; the corona represents the crown of thorns or the halo of glory; the lobed leaves, the hands, and the coiled tendrils the scourges of those who persecuted Him.

CULTURE: Most species and hybrids stand occasional sharp frost but they do best in areas which have mild winters. Plant them in full sunshine. They should be provided with a strong fence or trellis as a support. When cut to the ground by frost they often grow out again quickly in spring and flower by summer. In some regions it may be necessary to spray plants against caterpillars. Mature plants will survive long periods with little water. They do well in poor stony ground. Rich soil may result in over-vigorous stem and leaf growth, and few flowers.

P. x 'Allardii'

A frost-resistant plant with tremendous vitality which has to be cut back at least once a year to keep it from encompassing neighbouring plants. The large, ivory-white flowers appear in summer.

P. antioquiensis

This species from Colombia has two kinds of leaves – long and slender ones and others deeply cut into three lobes. The flowers hang down gracefully and are of a rich rose colour with a narrow violet corona. These are followed by long oval yellow fruits. It stands moderate frost.

P. caerulea — BLUE PASSION FLOWER

A Brazilian species which is rampant and needs regular trimming to keep it from straying too far and wide. The leaves have five to seven lobes and the flowers are cream, tinged with bluish-mauve or pink, with a corona shaded from blue at the tips to purple at the base. They are followed in autumn by inedible, ovoid, orange fruits. It is hardy to fairly severe frost, but in cold gardens it may shed most of its leaves in winter. 'Constance Elliott' is a fine cultivar with ivory flowers.

P. cinnabarina

An Australian species of rapid growth which reaches a height of 6 m or more, if not trimmed. The leaves are broad and wrinkled and the flowers rather elegant in form – with slender segments of cinnabar-red.

P. edulis — PURPLE GRANADILLA

An evergreen which grows quickly to 6 m and has a mass of handsome three-lobed leaves of rich green, and white flowers with a corona banded with deep purple. The oval fruits which are purple when ripe, are delicious in puddings, fruit salads and iced drinks. It needs long hot summers to encourage the production of fruit.

P. jamesonii
Is a romping, lusty evergreen with glossy leaves and flowers of salmon to coral-red in summer. Useful as a quick cover on a large fence or bank.

P. manicata   RED PASSION FLOWER
Is the most decorative of the passion flowers. It is an evergreen with dainty three-lobed leaves and tightly coiled tendrils like little springs. In summer and autumn it produces flowers of rich coral to cherry red, with a corona of deep blue making a colourful contrast. Cut back when necessary to prevent it from smothering neighbouring plants and forming a tangled mass. Once established it stands quite considerable frost.

P. mollissima   BANANA GRANADILLA
This is an invasive evergreen plant suitable for the large garden, to cover an ugly outbuilding or rubbish dump. It can become a problem if planted near trees or shrubs as it clambers all over them. Flowers of pink to rose festoon it in summer. These are followed by ovoid yellow fruits which are edible but not as tasty as those of *P. edulis*.

P. racemosa   RED PASSION FLOWER
(*P. princeps*)
A handsome evergreen Brazilian species with three-lobed leaves and a tendency to grow quickly. Flowers of coral-red with a corona of purple and white make a gay show in summer. Trim hard at least once a year to keep it within bounds.

PETREA VOLUBILIS   PURPLE WREATH,
        PETREA
DESCRIPTION: This native to Mexico and Central America is one of the most spectacular of the climbing plants which flower in early spring. The first flowers open when wisteria is reaching the end of its flowering period and the two standing near each other make a captivating show. In warm districts petrea will grow fairly quickly to 6 m or more, but in regions with cool winters it is slow in growth and may take several years to produce an abundance of flowers. It is a semi-evergreen which can be trimmed to shrub size or encouraged to grow upwards and tied to a support, or attached to a wall. The leaves are oval, of a delicate green when young but somewhat leathery and untidy when mature. The flowers appear in a glorious and sumptuous profusion. Each one consists of a corolla of five petals of lavender-purple nestling in a halo formed by the calyx which is of a paler shade. The plant has few leaves when it starts flowering and the flowers therefore show up clearly against a wall or the sky. They are carried in graceful drooping sprays. There is also a form with white flowers but it is not as spectacular as the species described.
CULTURE: Although this pretty climber does best in warm frost-free regions it will flower in districts which experience occasional sharp frosts if it is grown against an east or north-facing wall, or on a protected patio. It needs strong light to promote good flowering.

PHAEDRANTHUS BUCCINATORIUS
(*Bignonia cherere*)   MEXICAN BLOOD TRUMPET,
        RED TRUMPET VINE
DESCRIPTION: Most of the older generation still refer to this plant as *Bignonia cherere*, and perhaps this will remain its name amongst gardeners for years to come, as the new name is both ponderous and ugly. It is a handsome evergreen and a strong-grower which climbs by means of tendrils to 9 m or more, if it is not trimmed back occasionally. The leaves are made up of two oval leaflets about 9 cm in length. From spring to autumn it bears clusters of magnificent large trumpet-shaped flowers of a luminous coral-red, flushed with yellow in the throat. The plant needs a strong support to keep it erect. It can be trained along a fence to form a hedge, over a large pergola or patio for shade or shelter, against the walls of the house, or up into a tree. The foliage, its vigorous habit, its ability to cling to a support, the beauty of the flowers, and its long flowering period make this a most desirable climber for a large garden. It can, of course, be grown in a small garden but be ready to head it back before it starts to cover the roof. Such trimming may be necessary two or three times a year.
CULTURE: Plant it in rich soil and water it abundantly until it is well grown. In areas which have sharp frosts for long periods, plant it against a warm wall of the house. In regions where winters are mild, prune the plant back fairly hard each year after flowering is over, to keep it under control. It does best in full sun but in hot gardens inland it grows well also in partial shade.

Plant the Red Passion Flower (*Passiflora manicata*) for quick cover in a large garden.

Mexican Blood Trumpet (Phaedranthus) displaying its vivid flowers high up in a tree.

Petrea is a most rewarding climber to highlight the garden from early to mid-spring.

Plumbago tolerates difficult growing conditions and can easily be trained as a climber.

PHASEOLUS CARACALLA   Snail Vine

DESCRIPTION: An evergreen or deciduous climber which looks rather like a runner bean in growth and foliage. It climbs to 3 m or more and has its unusual flowers in late spring and summer. The coiled keel of the flower looks like a snail which accounts for its common name. The sweetly-scented flowers are cream combined with purple or mauve in colour. The plant can be grown as a ground cover, or against a wall or a trellis to form a screen.

CULTURE: Snail vine grows with cheerful abandon in warm regions but sharp frost may kill off the top-growth. When frosted down to the ground it often grows up quickly to flower again in summer. In districts which have cold winters it is advisable to plant it against a wall and to protect the roots with a mulch. It grows rapidly from seed sown in spring. Soak the seed in warm water for a few hours to speed up germination.

PHILODENDRON   Philodendron

DESCRIPTION: These are not true climbers but rather plants with stems which elongate and which can be used as climbers. Many species are grown as indoor plants because of the beauty of their leaves. Only two of the species which will grow out-of-doors are described here. They look effective against the trunk of a large tree where they give the impression of being part of a tropical jungle. Planted in a container they will not become very large and are ornamental on a shady patio or balcony, or in a large courtyard.

CULTURE: Plant in soil rich in humus, in shade or partial shade and protect from hot dry winds. These plants come from tropical regions and they cannot stand severe cold or dryness. The stems often produce aerial roots. A piece of stem with its rootlets will form a new plant, to take the place of older ones which may become leggy with age.

P. scandens

A very fast-growing philodendron generally propagated as an indoor plant. It has a slender stem and pretty mid-green leaves which are broadly heart-shaped at the base with a sharply pointed apex. It is suitable only for subtropical gardens as it needs a warm humid atmosphere.

Port St. John's Climber (*Podranea ricasoliana*). A robust climber for summer colour.

In summer Silver Lace Vine (*Polygonum aubertii*) bears a foaming mass of tiny flowers.

P. selloum
This is the hardiest of the philodendrons and the best to plant outside in the garden or on a large terrace or patio. It needs a support, but later develops a stout stem, and has huge and handsome, deeply incised leaves, which are ornamental throughout the year. It does best in partial shade but can be grown in full sunshine and it tolerates moderate frost.

PILEOSTEGIA VIBURNOIDES   PILEOSTEGIA
DESCRIPTION: An evergreen climber which occurs in eastern Asia. It has the merit of being hardy to severe frost and it is a self-clinging plant and not rampant in growth and therefore does not require much trimming and training to keep it neat and within bounds. It grows to about 6 m in height and bears glossy, slender, leathery leaves, from which emerge panicles of tiny ivory flowers in summer.
CULTURE: Pileostegia does well in mediocre soil and in full sun. Young plants need regular watering to promote development but established plants will endure fairly long periods of drought.

PLUMBAGO   PLUMBAGO
DESCRIPTION: The species described below are scandent shrubs rather than true climbers but, where conditions favour their growth, they can be trimmed and trained to make a pretty show against a wall, around a pillar or over a trellis. They also look attractive scrambling or rambling over an old tree trunk or a large boulder.
CULTURE: They do best in warm frost-free gardens, but can be grown in regions which have mild frost. The South African species is the hardier of the two, standing temperature drops to –3°C and long periods with little water, and dry wind.

P. auriculata   PLUMBAGO
(*P. capensis*)
Sends up numerous stems from ground level. They are pliable and covered with soft green leaves. Cut some of the stems out at the base and train the longer ones up against the wall or over a trellis. In summer it becomes festooned with clusters of sky-blue flowers which make a lovely show. There is a form with white flowers but it is not nearly as pretty as the blue. This South African plant makes an excellent hedge and it can also be trimmed in the form of a ball or cone.

P. rosea   PINK PLUMBAGO
Is native to the East Indies and is of twining habit. It reaches a height of about 2 m and bears delightful clusters of candy-pink flowers in summer. Water well during dry periods of the year.

PODRANEA BRYCEI   ZIMBABWE CREEPER
DESCRIPTION: A fast-growing climber from the warm regions of southern Africa. It will reach a height of 9 m unless trimmed from time to time. The plant is almost deciduous in cold gardens but evergreen in warm ones. It has leaves divided into decorative oval, pointed leaflets with serrated edges. The bignonia-like flowers are of a delightful shade of pink etched with rose stripes and marked with pale yellow in the throat. They are carried in very large clusters which make a splendid show in summer. *P. ricasoliana* (Port St. John's Climber) is very similar with flowers of lighter pink. These are climbers for quick cover in a large garden. Train them over the carport or any ugly outbuilding, or up a large bank. Their thick stems and their powerful growth make them unsuitable for a small garden.
CULTURE: Although partial to warmth, they will survive moderate frost and long periods with little water. Trim them each year in late winter to keep them neat. They do well in coastal gardens and inland where winters are mild.

POLYGONUM   SILVER LACE VINE
DESCRIPTION: Quick-growing deciduous climbers, rampant but graceful in growth, and quite sensational in late spring and early summer when they become a foaming mass of flowers. They can be used as ground cover, or as a screen against a fence, or to hide any unsightly object. They make a wonderful show trained up a dead tree trunk or along the netting enclosing a tennis court. The leaves are soft, arrow- or heart-shaped at the base and pointed at the apex. The plant drapes itself over a bank or twines around any handy support.
CULTURE: These hardy plants are able to stand intense cold and, when established, they also endure long periods with little water. They do better in cool gardens than in tropical ones. If they are not thinned out or cut back the plants tend to become untidy and outgrow their allotted space. Their rate of growth and how often they will need trimming depends on climatic conditions.

P. aubertii   Silver Lace Vine

A quick-growing effervescent deciduous climber which will reach 12 m if it is not trimmed back. It has pretty little leaves, and in late summer and early autumn it is wreathed in frothy clouds of small cream flowers. If the plant is placed near, or on the wall of the house it should be cut back hard after flowering, as otherwise it will grow over the roof.

P. baldschuanicum   Bokhara Vine,
                                    Russian Vine

This species, native to Turkey, is very similar to the one described above but the flowers, tinged with pink, are larger in size and carried in more substantial clusters. It is an exuberant plant growing 3–4 m in a year and finally attaining a height of 12 m, if not trimmed. The flowering time is summer.

PORANA PANICULATA   Snow Creeper

DESCRIPTION: An evergreen Indian plant with a climbing, twining nature. During the cool months of the year it produces an astonishing show – with its myriads of white flowers. Each bell-shaped flower is only about 1 cm long but they are carried in large foaming trusses which make an impressive sight. They have a faint vanilla-like scent. The leaves are heart-shaped and 6–10 cm long. Plant it where it can tumble over a wall or drape it around a pillar. Under optimum conditions it will grow to 6–10 m.

CULTURE: A quick-growing plant in a warm garden. It is susceptible to frost and is damaged by hot dry wind. Tie it to a support to keep it erect and thin out stems to prevent it from becoming a tangled mass.

PYROSTEGIA VENUSTA   Golden Shower,
(*Pyrostegia ignea*)   Orange Trumpet Creeper

DESCRIPTION: Where climatic conditions suit it this Brazilian climber puts on a sensational show in autumn and winter. It is an evergreen with oval pointed leaves which are dark green and slightly glossy. It grows to 6 m and more, and supports itself by means of tendrils. The bright orange tubular flowers make vivid curtains of colour for many weeks of the year, at a time when the deciduous plants in the garden are bare of leaves. Train it over an arbour or pergola, over a trellis to shade a patio, against the walls of the house,

along a fence to form a hedge, or let it clamber into a tree, or scramble over the ground to form a ground cover on a large bank.

CULTURE: This plant will grow and flower well where winters are not severe. Once established it will also endure long periods with little water but it should be watered well in autumn and winter to encourage flowering. In regions which have severe frost it can often be grown successfully on a north-facing wall or when planted where the early morning winter sun will not strike the plants. Prune every second year to keep it within bounds.

QUAMOCLIT LOBATA
(*Mina lobata*)

DESCRIPTION: A charming, quick-growing Mexican twiner which will romp up a pillar or post, or cover a trellis or fence in a matter of 3–4 months. It is erect rather than spreading in growth and, if colour is needed against a wall or fence, it is advisable to set out several plants about 60 cm apart. The apple-green, three-lobed leaves are attractive on their own, and the spikes of flowers which appear in summer are bright and cheerful. They are crimson when they open, changing through orange to yellow as they mature and fade. In a warm garden it may grow for several years, but under cold conditions it dies back, and it is therefore best regarded as a climber of temporary value to provide quick cover and colour whilst the slower ones develop. The flowers are useful for arrangements, as well as being decorative in the garden.

CULTURE: Set out plants in late winter or spring as soon as the weather is warm. Seed sown in spring will also produce flowering plants by summer. Soak seed for a day before sowing to speed up germination. It grows well in a hot, sunny position, but it should not be exposed to strong searing wind.

QUISQUALIS INDICA   Rangoon Creeper

DESCRIPTION: A quick-growing twiner which may reach a height of about 4 m in two years. It has broadly ovate leaves and sweetly-scented flowers which vary in colour, changing as they open and age, from white through pink to rose. Each flower consists of a long slender tube opening to a starry face of five petals. They are carried in clusters which hang down all over the plant and make a delightful show, particularly in summer.

A good plant for a quick screen.

CULTURE: This climber from tropical Africa and Asia thrives in warm humid conditions. It is a rampant grower and should be trimmed back annually to keep it within bounds and to prevent the plants from becoming straggly. In areas with mild frosts protect the plants in their first three years. Not recommended for cold gardens.

RHAPHIDOPHORA AUREA   IVY ARUM,
(*Scindapsus aureus*)   PATHOS

DESCRIPTION: An evergreen plant from the Solomon Islands grown for the beauty of its leaves. When young they are broadly ovate and bright green splashed with yellow. As they mature they turn darker in colour, enlarge to 30 cm or more in length, and become heart-shaped at the base with deeply cut margins. The plant has aerial roots which help it to support itself and from which new plants can be propagated. Grow it against a wall or tree for support. This is a decorative plant for a terrace or for inside the house. It will reach a height of 2 m when grown in a container and considerably more in the garden.

CULTURE: Thrives under sub-tropical conditions. It can, however, stand occasional mild frost. Plant in partial shade, in humus-rich soil and water regularly.

Rangoon Creeper (*Quisqualis indica*) grows quickly and flowers profusely in a warm humid climate.

The Fuchsia-flowering Currant (*Ribes speciosum*)

Wild Grape (*Rhoicissus tomentosa*) has lovely leaves.

Golden Shower (*Pyrostegia venusta*) wears its glowing mantle from early autumn to late winter.

RHODOCHITON ATROSANGUINEUM

(*R. volubile*)   PURPLE BELLS

DESCRIPTION: A climbing Mexican plant which supports itself by means of the leaf stalks which twine themselves around any support. It grows to about 3 m and makes a pretty show in a pot or in the garden. The leaves are heart-shaped and sparsely toothed. The flower consists of a large, flaring, rose to crimson calyx from which emerges a long tubular dark purple corolla. The flowering time is late spring or summer.

CULTURE: This plant should be regarded as an annual to provide a quick screen in the new garden or to grow in a container to enhance a patio. It grows readily from seed sown in spring and will flower in three to four months.

RHOICISSUS TOMENTOSA

WILD GRAPE, MONKEY ROPE

DESCRIPTION: A South African forest climber grown for its foliage. It is an evergreen which twines and clings to any available support. The round leaves are indented and somewhat like those of a grapevine in form, but of a richer texture. They are dark green and glossy on the upper surface and paler on the underside. The new growth and leaves are lustrous and covered with silky coppery hairs. Under forest conditions it produces fruit suitable for making a preserve. Train it around a pillar or let it make its way up into a tree or spread across the ground. In the small garden plant it in a container which will restrict its growth or cut it back each year to limit its spread. It can also be grown indoors as a house plant.

CULTURE: Grows in sun but prefers some shade. Once established it will tolerate moderate frost.

RIBES SPECIOSUM

FUCHSIA-FLOWERING CURRANT

DESCRIPTION: This species, native to California, is inclined to sprawl and become bushy unless it is trimmed and trained to a support. It is an evergreen plant which grows to 2 m and is the most ornamental of the flowering currants. The stems are pliable and armed with sharp bristles which make this an effective plant to grow as a barrier. The ovate to obovate leaves are deeply lobed and mid-green in colour. In late winter and early spring it bears graceful drooping strings of fuchsia-like flowers with long, protruding stamens.

CULTURE: It will grow in poor soil, but to encourage quick healthy development plant it in soil rich in humus and water well until it is two or three years old, after which it will tolerate fairly long periods with little water. It is hardy to sharp frost.

ROSA

ROSE

DESCRIPTION: Climbing roses may be divided into two broad groups: (1) The wichuraianas or ramblers and related species and cultivars, and (2) the climbers which have evolved from bush roses. The former generally have small flowers carried in clusters whilst the latter have flowers similar to the bush roses from which they have evolved. For example, climbing 'Peace' will have flowers just like the bush rose known as 'Peace'.

Both types make a pretty show when they bloom. The climbers produce their greatest profusion of flowers in mid-spring, but they bear a few blooms also in summer and autumn. The ramblers flower later in spring than do the climbers and, with a couple of exceptions, they do not flower again until the following spring.

Climbing roses may be trained up around a pillar but they produce more flowers if the canes are trained out horizontally along a wall or fence than when they are tied up to a pillar. For fences, plant them 3 metres apart and fan the stems out laterally as they develop. Ramblers look lovely scrambling over a fence or bank, making a ground cover, or twined around a pillar or over a pergola.

CULTURE: All roses are deciduous and hardy to severe cold. In fact they do better where winters are cold than in gardens where winters are mild. If the soil in the garden is not fertile make holes at least 60 cm wide and deep, and put into them an abundance of good compost and old manure. Roses like to be well watered and well fed. Fertilise them two or three times a year between late winter and late summer. Use a fertiliser specially prepared for roses, or a general garden fertiliser. Where water is in short supply plant fewer roses, as one plant adequately watered will produce more flowers than two which are not watered sufficiently. The best time to plant roses is during winter when they are dormant. They can, however, be planted out when in leaf, if they are established in containers which can be moved from the nursery to the garden without disturbing the roots of the growing plants.

The pruning of climbing roses should be done towards the end of winter. It is a simple task. During their first three years they may need no pruning at all, but, when their canes are long, cut off about 30–60 cm. Old climbers, which have been neglected and have many canes coming up from the ground or from near the ground, will require more drastic pruning, because, if all the canes are left there will be too many side shoots bearing flowers, with the result that the flowers will be very small.

When a climbing rose is four or more years old, and if it has a number of canes, cut out some of the older ones leaving the plant with four to six coming up from the ground. Never prune these remaining canes hard. After trimming back the tips set about pruning the side shoots which come off the main canes. Cut them back to within a couple of eyes of the main canes and they will throw out flowering shoots in spring which will bear blooms of good quality. When pruning roses or cutting flowers for the house, cut just above an eye or growth-bud.

Ramblers are not pruned in winter but in late spring, after they have flowered, and not until they are two or three years old. Cut out the old stems which have flowered, near ground level, leaving the young ones to grow on and bear flowers the following year. If numerous other gardening chores prevent you getting around to pruning the ramblers, do not be perturbed. They will produce masses of flowers when completely neglected and left unpruned for a couple of years, but they then may have taken over a great deal of the garden and prove difficult to untangle.

Pests and diseases: Well-nourished roses survive the attacks of a variety of pests and diseases. Most of the pests which attack roses are seasonal. They often disappear on their own in time, before they have done much damage. If necessary, procure the proper pesticide and use it according to directions on the container.

Scale is probably the most universal and most damaging of the pests. It appears on the stems as very small reddish brown scabs which are easily scratched off with the finger nail. These insects will be found associated with ants which encourage their spread. Spraying the roses with a strong mixture of lime-sulphur two or three times in mid-winter generally rids the plants of scale insects. Mix the lime-sulphur in the proportion of one of lime-sulphur to ten of water and spray once or twice when the roses are dormant, before pruning and again after pruning, at intervals of a week to ten days. Once the roses shoot, a spray as strong as this could kill off the new shoots, whilst a weaker mixture would do little to kill the scale. Should scale persist after the application of lime-sulphur in winter, try one of the proprietary brands of sprays made for scale, during the summer months.

Black spot is the most damaging disease which attacks roses. An afflicted plant has black spots or yellowish splodges on the leaves and, if the disease is not checked, the leaves fall off and the plant may die as a result. The spores over-winter in the ground and invade the plant tissues during warm humid weather. There are many sprays available to combat black spot. In districts where this disease is prevalent, and during periods of warm damp weather, spray the rose plants regularly once a fortnight with a suitable fungicide. Most of the fungicides now produced also help to prevent rust, which attacks roses and other plants under similar climatic conditions. It appears on the backs of the leaves in the form of tiny rusty pinpoint size spots.

Mildew is another fungus disease which can be troublesome during warm damp weather. The ends of shoots and the leaves become covered with a whitish-looking powder, and the tips of the leaves tend to curl up. A dusting with sulphur or an appropriate fungicide at intervals of two weeks will stop the spread of mildew and help the affected plants. This is not necessary with roses such as 'Dorothy Perkins' which invariably get mildew, but their flowering and growth is not adversely affected by it.

The following are the names of some very good ramblers and climbers. Climbers are preceded by the letters 'Cl'. The names of many others will be found in nursery catalogues.

'Albertine'	A rambler which grows to 5 m and has strong canes and double blooms of coppery pink. It is an old favourite with a rich scent.
'Banksia Roses'	Charming in mid-spring when they bear a glorious profusion of yellow or white flowers like little rosettes. They are faintly fragrant and carried in clusters on almost thornless stems.

The Macartney Rose (*Rosa bracteata*) makes a glorious show early in spring.

A rambler rose looks delightful cascading over a wall or steep bank.

'Dorothy Perkins' is recommended for decorating a fence or providing ground cover.

'Blaze' is the most richly coloured of the scarlet climbing roses.

A pergola adorned with different climbers is a fine feature for the large garden.

'Blaze'	A vigorous rambler with large clusters of semi-double flowers of vivid crimson.
'Bonfire'	A rambler which makes a splendid show in mid-spring when it is wreathed in myriads of crimson flowers.
'Cl. Caroline Testout'	An old cultivar with strongly scented, double, rose-pink flowers.
'Cl. Cecile Brunner'	Is a robust plant with tiny shell-pink buds carried in loose clusters. The flowers are splendid for miniature arrangements.
'Chaplin's Pink'	This is a good climber to plant against the wall of a house. It has bright pink flowers in great profusion.
'Cl. Charles Mallerin'	A handsome climbing rose for the large garden. Its flowers are a rich, velvet red with a delightful fragrance.
'Cl. Charlotte Armstrong'	This climber bears flowers with long, elegant buds of carmine-red.
'Cl. Circus'	Bears charming flowers flushed with different colours – red, yellow, orange and pink.
'Cl. Clair Matin'	Has semi-double flowers of shell-pink. It is a strong grower.
'Cl. Concerto'	A vigorous climber with scarlet flowers carried in large trusses.
'Coral Dawn'	A rambling rose growing to 5 m with lovely clusters of fragrant rose-pink flowers.
'Crepuscule'	This delightful rambler was introduced more than 50 years ago, and it is one of the few which flower again and again from spring to winter. It can be used as a hedge, around a pillar or as a shrub. The flowers are fairly small and of a delicate shade of apricot.
'Cl. Crimson Glory'	Is a climbing sport of the bush rose of the same name, with richly-scented, velvety, blood-red flowers of beautiful form.
'Crimson Shower'	A good rambler for training around a pillar or over an arch. It has small crimson flowers in large clusters.
'Dorothy Perkins'	An old favourite rambler for any part of the garden. Its massed clusters of pale pink flowers are a great joy towards the end of spring.
'Excelsa'	A vigorous rambler with masses of brilliant orange flowers in small clusters.
'Cl. Frensham'	A strong plant with clusters of flowers of medium size, of a deep crimson hue.
'Golden Showers'	Bears scented flowers of pale gold on long stems. The leaves are glossy and the stems almost thornless.
'Cl. Goldilocks'	Produces pretty clusters of canary-yellow flowers on strong-growing plants.
'Cl. High Noon'	An erect-growing rose with flowers of a dark canary-yellow hue.
'Cl. Iceberg'	Is like the bush rose of the same name with well-shaped white buds in clusters.
'Cl. King's Ransom'	A robust climber with flowers of deep golden-yellow.
'Macartney Rose'	Has pleasing foliage and large single snow-white flowers with golden anthers.
'Cl. Maria Callas'	Bears huge carmine flowers on strong stems.

'Mermaid'	This is an old favourite which grows vigorously to 6 m or more. It is almost evergreen and bears scented creamy-yellow single flowers measuring almost 10 cm across.
'New Dawn'	A rambler with shiny foliage and large double flowers of shell-pink.
'Cl. Orange Triumph'	Bears huge clusters of orange-scarlet flowers. This is a vigorous plant.
'Paul's Lemon Pillar'	Bears masses of small pale yellow flowers with a delicate fragrance.
'Paul's Scarlet'	A sensational plant when in full bloom with tight clusters of crimson flowers.
'Cl. Peace'	The climber bears the same beautifully formed roses of palest yellow flushed with pink which made the bush rose popular.
'Cl. Queen Elizabeth'	A vigorous climber with flowers of pale pink. They last well in arrangements.
'Royal Scarlet'	A rambler for arbours and arches, with clusters of brilliantly red flowers.
'Cl. Super Star'	Bears medium sized flowers of a glowing coral colour, like the bush rose with the same name.
'Tausendschön'	An old rambler which remains popular; it has glossy foliage and clusters of rose-pink flowers.
'Veilchenblau'	An old type of rambler rose with mauve buds which open to deeper mauve flowers with a pale centre. Fine for an arch or pergola.
'Cl. Zambra'	Bears trusses of flowers of sunset colours. Splendid when in full bloom.
'Zéphirine Drouhin'	One of the old-fashioned climbers with thornless stems of light green foliage and semi-double carmine flowers with a rich fragrance.

SARITAEA MAGNIFICA   SARITAEA
(*Bignonia magnifica*)

DESCRIPTION: This is a vigorous evergreen climber from the subtropical region of South America. Its lustrous leaves are somewhat leathery in texture, obovate in form and 6–10 cm long. They are usually arranged in pairs. In spring and on and off during other seasons it carries clusters of handsome funnel-shaped flowers 6–8 cm long and 4–6 cm across. They are deep mauve to amethyst with lighter streaks in the throat. Under congenial conditions it will grow to 10 m but it is easy to keep it under control. This is a handsome plant better suited to the large garden than the small one.
CULTURE: Saritaea flourishes in warm gardens but it will grow well also in regions where frosts are never more than mild. Water the plant well during the winter to ensure good spring flowering.

SCHIZOPHRAGMA   CLIMBING HYDRANGEA
DESCRIPTION: This genus belongs to the same family as the common hydrangea and bears some resemblance to it. The plant climbs by means of aerial roots which support the stems by sticking to the surface of a wall or to the bole of a tree. Two species are worth trying where conditions are favourable to their growth. Both are deciduous and bloom in summer.
CULTURE: They need soil rich in humus, plenty of water, and shade. These plants are not suitable for gardens subject to hot dry winds or subtropical conditions.

S. hydrangeoides
Grows to 6 m and has foliage very like that of the hydrangea, broadly ovate and coarsely toothed. The flowerheads, up to 25 cm across, are made up of small flowers of creamy-white. It occurs in nature in forests in Japan.

S. integrifolia
A Chinese species which may reach a height of 9 m under suitable conditions. The leaves are large and the flowerheads more ornamental than

'Crepuscule'. An old favourite, with masses of small roses on and off from spring to autumn.

Plant rambler roses to form a hedge which is colourful in spring and impenetrable at all times.

the species described above. They may be 30 cm in diameter and the individual flowers are also much larger and make a better show.

SENECIO
CANARY CREEPER,
MEXICAN FLAME CLIMBER

DESCRIPTION: There are many different types of senecio. It is one of the largest genera of flowering plants in the world but only a few are decorative climbers. These are good plants to grow where quick cover is required. They make a pretty screen and look charming when grown over a trellis or pergola, on a patio, over a tree stump, or as ground cover. The leaves vary considerably in shape, size and colour – the flowers are daisy-like in form.

CULTURE: Although they may be cut down to the ground by frost, they will often emerge again in spring and grow rapidly to flower once more by summer or autumn. In areas where frost is common plant them in a protected position. Not recommended for areas of severe frost. They do well in sun or partial shade and are good plants for coastal gardens.

S. confusus
MEXICAN FLAME CLIMBER

In warm areas it is an evergreen. Where winters are cool it loses most of its leaves. The slender twining stems grow to 3 m and bear roughly toothed leaves up to 10 cm in length and about 2 cm in width. They are somewhat fleshy and light green in colour. It starts flowering in late spring and the daisy-like flowers of bright orange make a spectacular show until late autumn. Train it along a fence or let it spill over a bank or over the edge of a tub. Trim plants after flowering is over to keep them neat.

S. macroglossus
CAPE IVY

Is a South African plant with lustrous, rather fleshy triangular leaves shaped like those of ivy, and pretty yellow daisies about 4 cm across, carried singly. This species is not as showy as the others but it is a useful plant to trail over a bank, to grow as a ground cover, or to train up a small support to form a verdant background. It is quick-growing to 2–3 m and stands fairly sharp frost.

S. mikanioides
GERMAN IVY

This South African species is seldom grown in its own country but is cultivated in the northern

The huge flowers of Cup of Gold (*Solandra maxima*) have a vanilla-like scent.

Canary Creeper (*Senecio tamoides*). A fast-grower which produces a curtain of flowers in autumn.

hemisphere as an indoor plant or to embellish a container on a terrace or patio. In a mild climate it will grow rapidly to a height of 4 m and twine itself about any available support. It is an evergreen with pretty, mid-green leaves with five to seven sharply pointed lobes – rather like those of an ivy. In summer and early autumn it bears heads of small yellow flowers with no ray florets. A cultivar with variegated leaves is useful for the small garden as it is not vigorous or invasive.

S. tamoides   CANARY CREEPER
This species from the southern part of Africa flowers at the same time as the Mexican flame climber. Planted next to each other they produce a scintillating show. Its soft, light green leaves shaped rather like those of the ivy, are attractive throughout the year. The plant which grows to 3–5 m or more makes a pretty screen and looks effective, too, against a wall or on a trellis. It will stand fairly long periods with little water and some frost, and it grows in full sun or part shade. The large clusters of yellow daisy flowers are bright and cheerful in late summer and early autumn. They have a delightful aromatic scent. It is very quick-growing and should be trimmed back regularly to prevent it taking over too much of the garden.

SOLANDRA   CUP OF GOLD
DESCRIPTION: Three vigorous climbers which need space for the development of their powerful limbs are included in this genus. They have handsome, somewhat lustrous and slightly leathery, oval, pointed leaves which are of ornamental value throughout the year. The young stems need some support but as the plant grows it becomes sturdy enough to support itself. In a congenial climate the stems go on growing and can make their way up a six-storey building or along a fence to a distance of 60 m. Obviously these are not climbers for the small garden, although they are useful stop-gap plants which can be kept down to reasonable size by annual trimming after the flowers drop. The flowers are larger than those of any other plant described in this book. They are chalice-shaped with five frilled or reflexed segments, and measure up to 20 cm across and as much, or more, in length.
CULTURE: They flourish near the coast and do fairly well even where subjected to salt-laden wind. They grow very quickly in the interior too,

but are not hardy to sharp frost. Annual pruning of established plants is necessary to keep them from ranging too far and wide, and to encourage better flowering. Cut off faded flowers with a good length of stem, and, if the plant is still too large, remove a couple of stems near the base. Although tolerant of fairly long periods of drought they flower best when watered regularly.

S. grandiflora
Is native to the West Indies and has scented flowers which are amber to creamy-yellow with distinct maroon lines on the inside. The segments of the corolla are slightly frilled and not as reflexed as in the other species described.

S. longiflora   SOLANDRA
Is another West Indian species which does best in tropical and subtropical regions. This species has longer and more slender flowers than the other two. They are ivory when young and creamy-yellow as they mature, and have purple stripes running down the inside of the flower.

S. maxima   CUP OF GOLD
This name has now been given to the species previously known as *S. guttata*, *S. hartwegii* or *S. nitida*. This is the most handsome of the species and, being native to Mexico, it is also more tolerant of cold. It is a lusty climber with tremendous vitality, flamboyant and determined to lord it over all others by growing larger and at a quicker rate. The flowers are 10–20 cm long and up to 20 cm across, of a rich mustard-yellow colour with five maroon stripes running down the inside of the flower from the reflexed segments to the base of the corolla. They are bold and handsome in appearance and have a scent rather like a vanilla custard. A good plant to adorn a fence around a large property, or to train against a large expanse of bare wall. It looks out-of-place in the garden of moderate size. It survives moderate frost and wind.

SOLANUM   POTATO CREEPER,
                        COSTA RICAN NIGHTSHADE
DESCRIPTION: The genus includes deciduous and evergreen shrubs, trees and climbers as well as the potato. Descriptions of three of the most decorative climbing species are given below.
CULTURE: They are quick-growing plants which need little attention. Although tender to frost the

species described can be grown in gardens where frosts are not severe. If frost should cut them down to the ground they generally survive and grow up again quickly in spring and flower by summer.

S. crispum

A scandent shrub which sends out long pliable stems that can be trained against a wall or fence. It is semi-evergreen, losing most of its leaves in a cold winter. The flowers are similar to those of the potato, of a rich purple-blue, with a bright yellow central part. They appear in loose clusters in late spring and summer, and are followed by small round yellow fruits. It is useful for a fence or to have scrambling over a shed. It does well in alkaline soil and stands fairly severe frost.

S. jasminoides POTATO VINE

Is a strong and fast-growing, twining plant from South America which grows to 9 m. In regions of mild winters it is evergreen. The star-shaped flowers which measure 2–3 cm across are bluish-white with conspicuous golden anthers. They are carried in loose clusters in summer and autumn. There is also a form with white flowers. This twiner will stand fairly severe frosts. It should be cut back after flowering to keep it within bounds as otherwise it may take up too much of the garden, or become a tangled mass of growth. It is a useful stop-gap plant because of its eagerness to grow but it is not very ornamental.

S. wendlandii POTATO CREEPER
COSTA RICAN NIGHTSHADE

This is the most decorative climber belonging to this genus of plants. It sends up sturdy fast-growing twining stems to 8 m, and in late spring and summer it bears a profusion of large clusters of lavender-blue flowers which make quite a spectacular show. This species is generally deciduous. It does best where winters are mild but if grown against a north-facing wall it will survive in regions where temperatures drop to a little below freezing. When frosted it generally recovers very quickly and flowers again in summer. Established plants will stand a good deal of drought. This is a plant to provide summer shade on a trellis or arbour or to train around the pillars of a pergola or along a fence. Its stems tend to sprawl unless they are tied to a support. To ensure a neat appearance train and tie them to a support as they lengthen and cut the plant back somewhat after flowering.

SOLLYA FUSIFORMIS BLUEBELL CREEPER
(*S. heterophylla*)

DESCRIPTION: Is an evergreen native to Western Australia. It is not a particularly showy plant but worth trying where soil and climate make gardening difficult. It does not reach more than 2–3 m in height and has pliable, twining stems of small pale green leaves. In the warm months of the year it produces little blue, bell-shaped flowers which are followed in autumn by small purple berries. Plant it where it can spill down over a wall or bank or over the sides of a row of steps, or grow it in a container.

CULTURE: Established plants stand moderate frost and considerable drought but they flower best when watered fairly regularly.

STAUNTONIA HEXAPHYLLA
JAPANESE STAUNTON VINE

DESCRIPTION: An evergreen twining plant, exuberant in growth, which may reach 6 m or more. The new leaves are pale yellowish green, turning dark green as they mature. Each leaf is composed of 3–7 shining ovate leaflets which give the plant an attractive appearance. In late winter or early spring it carries clusters of white, scented, bell-shaped flowers. The plants are either male or female. Where both are growing near each other the female bears edible rosy fruits the size of a small plum. These make a prettier show than the flowers. Train the plant up a trellis or a wall, or allow it to form a ground cover.

CULTURE: Needs rich soil and plenty of water but, once established, it will survive fairly long periods of drought. Near the coast it grows in full sunshine. In hot inland gardens grow it in partial shade. Stands drops in temperature to below freezing. As the plant may look untidy if it is not cut back, trim it once a year in late summer.

STEPHANOTIS FLORIBUNDA
STEPHANOTIS, MADAGASCAR JASMINE

DESCRIPTION: A delightful twining evergreen plant which grows to 2–3 m. The handsome leaves are oval in form, dark green, thick and glossy and about 10 cm long. The flower consists of a tube flaring out to a starry face of five pointed segments. They are waxy-white and carried in loose clusters in spring and early summer. In addition to their elegant appearance they give off a sweet fragrance. They last well in arrangements and are perfect for

Plant a climber near the front door to decorate the entrance to the house.

wedding bouquets. This is a splendid climber to grow indoors or outdoors on a patio.

CULTURE: Madagascar jasmine will grow outside in a warm humid climate and is at its best in subtropical gardens. In other areas plant it in a pot which can be taken indoors when the weather becomes cool in autumn. It needs rich soil with plenty of humus. The roots of the plant should be shaded but the top can be in filtered sunlight. Protect it from intense sunshine and drying winds. This is not an easy plant to grow but it is worth taking some trouble to create the conditions which suit it.

STICTOCARDIA BERAVIENSIS

MADAGASCAR CONVOLVULUS

DESCRIPTION: A pretty evergreen climbing plant from Madagascar and the tropical regions of Africa, with large heart-shaped leaves. It is related to convolvulus and bears flowers which are somewhat similar in form. They appear in clusters, are funnel-shaped and beautifully coloured – a rich yellow at the base with cornelian-red at the mouth. In a congenial climate it is quick-growing, and a useful plant therefore for a new garden to provide a background whilst the slower plants take their time to develop. It grows from 6 to 9 m.

CULTURE: This is not a plant for cold gardens. It thrives under subtropical conditions and cannot stand frost and cold dry winds. Plant it in soil rich in humus and water well. It needs regular trimming to keep it within bounds.

STIGMAPHYLLON CILIATUM

GOLDEN VINE, ORCHID VINE, AMAZON VINE

DESCRIPTION: This slender twining plant is suitable for the small garden where space is limited, or for planting on a patio or terrace. It is an evergreen growing to 6 m and has delicate stems with soft, light green, heart-shaped leaves. The new growth which is of a shining coppery colour adds lustre to the plant in spring. In summer it bears dainty flowers in clusters. They are bright golden-yellow with petals which are prettily frilled around the edges. Grow it next to a low fence or near a post around which it can twine.

CULTURE: It needs soil rich in humus. In hot inland gardens plant it in partial shade. At the coast it will do well in the open. Established plants stand mild frost, but in a cool garden they should be planted in a sheltered spot.

Potato Creeper (Solanum wendlandii) will add colour to the garden in summer.

Golden Vine (Stigmaphyllon ciliatum) is a dainty climber with pretty leaves and flowers.

STRONGYLODON MACROBOTRYS
JADE VINE

DESCRIPTION: There is perhaps no more spectacular climber than the jade vine – a native to the Philippine Islands, where it can be found festooning the trees in the warm humid forests. In the right climate it develops into a woody climber of great vigour. The leaves divided into three, are dark green and slightly glossy. The flowers are carried closely clustered along the flowering stems – each inflorescence being 60 cm long. A mature plant with its skeins of flowers exquisitely shaded from sea-green to jade, is a most beautiful and impressive sight. The main flowering time is spring to summer. Train it over a patio or arbour, or across the pillars of a pergola. The pergola should have strong cross-beams and tall posts to support the weight of the plant and to make it possible for the long stems of flowers to hang down freely and be seen from the best angle. After the flowers fade it has large cylindrical seedpods.

CULTURE: A handsome plant for regions where warmth and humidity are high, but it may survive 2° of frost if the stems are protected. It should be planted in semi-shade and watered regularly during dry periods of the year to provide humidity in the air as well as in the soil. This plant, together with *Mucuna bennettii* from New Guinea, makes a splendid show in tropical gardens.

STROPHANTHUS GRATUS   ROUPELLIA
(*Roupellia grata*)

DESCRIPTION: In its native habitat, tropical west Africa, this plant is a vigorous climber, but in the garden it is unlikely to grow to more than 3 m and it tends to become bushy, unless excessive side-growth is cut out, and the remaining stems are trained along a support. It is an evergreen with long, shiny, dark green leaves and clusters of lightly-scented pink flowers made up of a tube with five reflexed rounded segments.

CULTURE: Suitable only for tropical and sub-tropical gardens at the coast and inland. Water well during dry periods of the year.

TECOMANTHE VENUSTA   TECOMANTHE
DESCRIPTION: Is a handsome evergreen climber from New Guinea. It is quick-growing but not too rampant for the small garden. Its glossy, dark green leaves are divided into three with the

The flowers of Jade Vine (*Strongylodon macrobotrys*) are carried in opulent trusses 60 cm long.

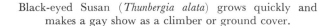

Black-eyed Susan (*Thunbergia alata*) grows quickly and makes a gay show as a climber or ground cover.

terminal leaflet larger than the other two. In spring it produces showy clusters of pendent tubular flowers of warm coral-red on the old wood. Plant it to ornament the terrace or patio. It does well as a container plant, and is perhaps best grown in this way in cold gardens as it can then be moved to a sheltered corner in winter.

CULTURE: This is a climber for a warm garden. Plant it in soil rich in humus, in partial shade, and water well during dry weather.

TECOMARIA CAPENSIS

CAPE HONEYSUCKLE

DESCRIPTION: A South African plant which is a shrub rather than a true climber or twiner, but its long pliable stems are easily trained horizontally along a fence or wall. Clipped regularly it makes a good hedge. Its foliage is attractive throughout the year. The leaves are divided into five to nine toothed oval dark green leaflets with a slight sheen. In late summer, when there is little in flower, it produces clusters of bright orange tubular flowers which make a lively show. There is also one with yellow flowers. It looks splendid planted near plumbago which has blue flowers at the same time.

CULTURE: Grows fairly quickly to 2–3 m. It is recommended for the large garden rather than the small as it requires space to develop. Established plants stand moderate frost and long periods with little or no water.

THUNBERGIA

BLACK-EYED SUSAN, ORANGE CLOCK VINE AND OTHERS

DESCRIPTION: These pretty climbers can be trained along a fence to form a hedge, or grown up the sides of a building, on a trellis, or over a pergola. They are very eager to grow and, once established, need little attention other than regular trimming to keep them within bounds. Descriptions are given under the species names.

CULTURE: The thunbergias described are evergreen or semi-evergreen plants, native to warm countries and they, therefore, naturally do best in tropical and subtropical gardens. When once established they will stand occasional fairly sharp frosts. Very often when cut down to the ground by frost they grow up quickly again in spring. Most of them like full sunshine. In cold districts plant thunbergias in a pot for use on a patio when in flower, and store them in a sheltered corner or a glasshouse during winter. They grow quickly when the weather has warmed up in spring.

T. alata
BLACK-EYED SUSAN

A gay, colourful, easy-to-grow twining evergreen plant from South Africa which rapidly covers any support handy – be it trellis, pillar, wall or other plants. It also drapes itself attractively over a hanging basket or tub and makes an effective ground cover. The heart-shaped leaves are about 7 cm long and the pretty flowers are composed of a short tube ending in a face of five spreading segments. The species is of a gaudy orange colour, effectively marked with black in the throat, which makes a striking contrast. Hybrids have flowers of yellow or white. In regions which have cold winters treat it as an annual. Where winters are mild, trim the plant after flowering is over to keep it within bounds, otherwise it will romp along happily over neighbouring plants. It does well in hot, dry areas.

T. coccinea
SCARLET CLOCK VINE

A robust climbing plant from India with large thick leaves with toothed margins. It bears long, drooping clusters of funnel-shaped flowers coloured orange in the throat, with flaring crimson lobes. This species will thrive only in warm gardens where it will grow to 3–6 m.

T. grandiflora
SKY FLOWER

Is a delightful twining plant which will grow to 4 m or more. Initially it may be slow but, once established, is fast-growing. The old leaves are somewhat tatty and it is advisable to cut back some stems each year to restrain the spread of the plant and to force new growth and new leaves which are of a soft, pleasant shade of green. They are heart-shaped at the base and as much as 15 cm in length. In summer and autumn it produces cascades of glorious lilac flowers, rather like those of a gloxinia in form. Plant it for shade over a patio, to cover a boundary fence, or let it scramble into a tall tree. It does best in a warm climate but withstands moderate frost. There is also one with white flowers which makes a good display in late summer, but it is not as splendid as the one with lilac flowers.

T. gibsonii
GOLDEN GLORY CREEPER,
(T. gregorii)
ORANGE CLOCK VINE

This species is exuberant in growth but can be

restrained by planting it in a container which will limit root-spread. It makes a vivid screen or hedge when trained over a fence or along a trellis, or it can be planted to form a scrambling ground cover, to cascade over a bank or low wall, or to embellish a tree stump or a patio. Gaudy orange trumpet-like flowers with unequal segments appear in spring and summer, and on and off during other seasons too. It stands quite severe frost but will be more successful if planted where it has some protection.

T. laurifolia   BENGAL TRUMPET
A Burmese species with long narrow leaves with clear veins. This plant attaches itself to a support by twining the leaf-stalks around it as does a clematis. The flowers are as beautiful as those of *T. grandiflora*, but the plant will succumb more readily to cold. A splendid species for a large subtropical garden.

T. mysorensis   Lady's Slipper
Is native to India, and in a warm climate it will grow rapidly to 6 m or more. It is an evergreen with leaves about 10 cm long, cuneate at the base and pointed at the tip. In autumn and winter, and on and off during other seasons, the plant is highlighted by pendent, cylindrical inflorescences 30–45 cm long. The buds are mahogany-red and the open flowers are composed of a curved tube of the same colour opening to a yellow mouth with recurved segments – rather like a lady's old-fashioned boot – which accounts for the common name.

TRACHELOSPERMUM JASMINOIDES

(*Rhynchospermum jasminoides*)   STAR JASMINE
DESCRIPTION: Star jasmine is an attractive evergreen twining plant to make a verdant curtain over a wall or bank, or to train on a pergola or arbour to provide shade beneath. It can be grown as ground cover in a large garden and it will also make a pretty show if trimmed to keep it to shrub size. The plant grows to 6 m and needs support on which to twine itself. The ovate, shining dark green leaves are about 5 cm in length, and show up to perfection the delicate white flowers which appear in spring and summer in loose clusters. Their enchanting fragrance and delicate beauty make this a rewarding plant. It can readily be identified by reason of the fact that the 5 petals are rolled back along their sides. In

hot inland gardens plant it where it is shaded for part of the day. *T. jasminoides* 'Variegatum' is not as rampant in growth and, therefore, better suited to the small garden. Its leaves are marked with white. *T. asiaticum* is another decorative plant, with smaller flowers, coloured cream to yellow. They have a rich, fruity fragrance.
CULTURE: When once established it will stand temperatures to —5°C. It will also tolerate considerable drought and is therefore a useful plant for regions where extremes make gardening difficult. Plant it in soil rich in humus to encourage fast initial growth. If it becomes too large cut back some of the old stems in autumn or winter.

TROPAEOLUM   CANARY BIRD VINE

DESCRIPTION: The genus includes the well-known and popular garden nasturtium as well as a few decorative climbers or twiners. They differ in appearance and are therefore more fully described under their species names.
CULTURE: Some species stand fairly severe frost but most of them do best where winters are mild and where adequate moisture is available. In regions where hot dry winds prevail plant them in partial shade. They do best in acid soil rich in humus.

T. peregrinum   CANARY BIRD VINE
A quick-growing climber from Peru which may reach a height of 3 m in a season. Although a perennial it is usually treated as an annual as young plants flower better than old ones. It looks delightful scrambling over a tree stump or a big boulder, or spilling over a low wall. The soft green leaves are deeply and prettily lobed. In summer it carries little canary-yellow flowers made up of unequal segments with frilled, incised edges. Where hot dry conditions prevail plant it in filtered shade.

T. polyphyllum   CANARY CREEPER
A trailing plant from Peru which sends up new growth each spring from a rhizome. It can be trained up a support or left to spread along the soil as a ground cover. The grey-green leaves are deeply cut into five lobes. In summer it bears a profusion of gay lemon-yellow flowers. It grows to 2–3 m in height. In a cold garden regard it as an annual or grow it in a container in a warm sheltered corner.

Golden Glory Creeper (*Thunbergia gibsonii*) grows with cheerful abandon even in poor soil.

The leaves of Star Jasmine (*Trachelospermum jasminoides*) are a perfect foil to its scented flowers.

Sky Flower (*Thunbergia grandiflora*) bears its enchanting flowers in summer and early autumn.

T. speciosum FLAME CREEPER

This is a small twiner from Chile which grows from a rhizome. It is a deciduous plant which dies down in autumn and bursts into new growth in spring. The pale green six-lobed leaves are most attractive from when they appear until autumn, and in late spring and early summer the plant is gay with nasturtium-like flowers of coral-red. Not recommended for gardens where hot dry winds blow. Plant in acid soil rich in humus, in partial shade, and water regularly.

T. tricolorum

A tuberous plant which sends up twining stems to 2 m in spring and summer, and dies down in autumn and winter. The clover-like leaves are prettily divided into five to seven lobes. Attractive spurred flowers appear in summer. The calyx is orange-red and the corolla is deep coral tipped with yellow.

T. tuberosum

Grows up rapidly in spring from its tuberous rootstock to a height of 3 m. The rounded, deeply cut, palmate leaves make a pleasing background to the long-spurred red and yellow flowers which decorate the plant in summer and autumn. The top growth then dies back until spring.

A grape vine will high-light the garden in autumn and provide a canopy of shade in summer.

Wisteria is a splendid climber to embellish the walls of a large house.

VITIS   GRAPE VINE AND OTHERS

DESCRIPTION: The genus includes the grape vine and other climbers, some of which are rather like a Virginia creeper. They do not bear attractive flowers but some species have leaves which are pretty in spring and summer and highly ornamental in autumn when they turn rich and varied colours. In some, the leaves are deeply incised into slender lobes whilst others have leaves and fruits like a grape vine. Most of them are vigorous in habit and can be trained to twine up into a tree, to curtain a wall, to cover an old stump, to climb posts or decorate the beams of a pergola, or to provide shade over a patio. They support themselves by twining or by their strong tendrils.

CULTURE: These plants are hardy to severe frost and, once established, they also survive fairly long periods of drought. They are not recommended for subtropical gardens as they do best where winters are cool to cold, and their leaves assume beautiful tints only in regions where autumnal weather is crisp. They will grow in slightly alkaline soil. Prune every year to keep plants from ranging too far afield.

V. amurensis   AMURLAND GRAPE,
                         SCARLET-LEAFED VINE

Is native to Manchuria. It grows to 12 m and its new growth is prettily coloured rose to crimson. The leaves are large, three- to five-lobed, and put on a splendid display in autumn when they turn bright shades of orange and red before dropping.

V. coignetiae   JAPANESE CRIMSON GLORY VINE

A robust climber which is spectacular in autumn. It will grow to 18 m if not cut back to keep it smaller. Let it grow into a tall tree or scramble over an unsightly outbuilding. The broad leaves may measure 30 cm across and have three to five lobes. The leaves are mid-green on the top surface and covered with rusty coloured hairs on the underside. In autumn they turn glorious shades from amber through pink and rose to a fiery crimson. It bears bunches of purple berries but these are inedible.

V. labrusca   FOX GRAPE

A North American species which grows to 6 m or a little more. The leaves are broad, heart-shaped at the base, with three lobes. They are rather thick, dark green above and covered with a rusty-brown felt on the underside. It bears small bunches of edible grapes with a musky flavour and

was used as a parent in the propagation of cultivated grapes in America.

V. vinifera   GRAPE VINE

The original species from which thousands of cultivars have originated is probably a native to Asia Minor and the region near the Caucasus. There are numerous named cultivars grown in different countries of the world, some for the making of wine and others for the table. Most of them colour slightly in autumn and some are spectacular at this season of the year. The following are the names of some of those known to be ornamental enough for a show in the garden:- 'Allicante Bouschet', 'Apiifolia', 'Brandt', 'Glory Vine', 'Grand Noir de la Calmette', 'Incana', 'Pontacq', 'Purpurea'. It is advisable to allow only one main stem to grow to the top of a pillar or arbour and to remove side shoots and basal growth below 1,5 m.

WISTERIA   WISTERIA

DESCRIPTION: This lovely deciduous climber has been grown for so long and in so many gardens that it needs no general description. It is a twining plant of exuberant growth, which will live for generations. Unsurpassed in vigour it will climb a tree to 20 m, or make its way up a support to the roof of a fairly high building. No flowering plant produces a greater abundance of glorious flowers in spring. The cascades of misty mauve or white lend an air of elegance to the garden, and their alluring scent pervades the garden and drifts into the house. Some gardeners avoid planting wisteria believing that the flowering period is short but, in fact, it wears its enchanting mantle of flowers for just as long as most of the other flowering plants.

It is a splendid plant to grow over an arbour or trellis, or across a patio, as in summer it provides a pretty canopy of shade and in winter it is bare of leaves and allows the sunshine to come through. If the plant is not cut back each year it will soon outgrow its space in the garden.

As a climber it can be grown along a fence to form a hedge or screen or it can be trained up an old, dead or living tree. A wisteria flowering in the branches of a crabapple, which flowers at the same time, is an unforgettable sight! It can be fastened to the walls of a house or to a strong trellis, pillar or post anywhere in the garden. It can also be trained to form a scandent shrub and it looks most effective when trained to form a weeping tree.

One should remember when planting a wisteria that the slender stem will, within a lifetime grow into a trunk 20 cm in diameter. To train a wisteria to form a weeping tree tie the stem to a stake of the desired height and remove side stems and growth buds which emerge from below. The plant should be allowed to have side stems only at the height at which it is to form a head, i.e. 3 m above the ground. Tie the main stem to the stake in several places to keep it straight, using something soft which will not bruise the stem. In the first winter the side stems which grow out from the head should be cut back to within a couple of eyes to thicken them.

Wisteria benefits from being cut back from time to time. Sometimes old plants bloom sparsely and it will generally be found that if the top-growth is cut back and some of the roots are severed, they will produce more flowers.

CULTURE: Wisteria generally grows with cheerful abandon in areas with very cold winters but does not do well in subtropical gardens. To encourage quick initial growth, plant it in acid soil rich in humus. Alkaline soil may lead to yellowing of the leaves and stunted growth. Where this happens treat the soil with sulphur or aluminium sulphate or spray the leaves with iron chelates. Young plants should be watered well during periods of dry weather. Mature plants will tolerate long periods without much water. They do well in partial shade. As severe frost late in the season may damage the flower buds it is advisable, where such frosts occur, to plant it where it is shaded from the early morning sun in winter.

W. floribunda   JAPANESE WISTERIA
(*W. multijuga*)
Japanese wisteria grows to 9 m or more. Trained to a high trellis, wall or pergola it will make a grand display. The trusses of flowers of this species measure as much as 30 cm in length. The individual flowers are smaller than those of Chinese wisteria and not as tightly clustered. They are jacaranda-blue in colour. Several cultivars are available:- 'Alba' with white flowers; 'Geisha' with flowers of palest blue; 'Macrobotrys' with trusses of deep mauve up to 1 m in length; 'Longissima Alba' – long trusses with white flowers; 'Rosea' with pink flowers tipped with purple; 'Violacea Plena' with flowers of violet-blue.

W. sinensis   CHINESE WISTERIA
This species is the noblest of climbers. It has broader trusses with flowers more closely arranged than the species described above. This is the species most often found in gardens in all parts of the world. It makes a spectacular display in a sunny or a shady garden. The flowers which appear before the new leaves, are of a rich shade of lavender-blue. The leaves, divided into numerous oval pointed leaflets, make a shady canopy of a soft green colour in summer and become a delightful shade of buttercup-yellow before dropping in autumn. The following cultivars are worth trying in the large garden:- 'Alba' (white flowers); 'Black Dragon' (double, dark purple) and 'Plena' (double, lilac). Old plants may cover 30 m or more and have a stem circumference of 1 m at ground level.

W. venusta   SILKY WISTERIA
The leaves of this species have silky hairs and the large white, scented flowers are carried in rather short sprays which are decorative when seen against a red brick wall or in front of a tree with very dark green leaves (e.g. pine). A cultivar of this species, known as 'Violacea', has flowers of violet-blue. It is more ornamental than the species and as vigorous in growth.

Planted at the base of a tree wisteria needs no additional form of support.

Wisteria interplanted with Golden Shower makes a cheerful picture in late winter.

This lovely cultivar of *Wisteria floribunda* has trusses of ivory tinged with palest lilac – almost a metre long.

Index of Common Names

Index of Botanical Names